AF560260

INDIA AND ASEAN IN THE 21ST CENTURY

INDIA AND ASEAN IN THE 21ST CENTURY

Economic Linkages

By
Sanjay Ambatkar

ANMOL PUBLICATIONS PVT. LTD.
NEW DELHI - 110 002 (INDIA)

ANMOL PUBLICATIONS PVT. LTD.
4374/4B, Ansari Road, Daryaganj
New Delhi - 110 002
Ph.: 3261597, 3278000
Visit us: www.anmolbooks.com

India and ASEAN in the 21st Century: Economic Linkages

First Edition, 2002

ISBN 81-261-1135-6

ICSSR Consultant: Dr. V. Suryanarayan

[The publication of this book is partially financed by the Indian Council of Social Science Research, New Delhi. However, the responsibility for the facts stated, conclusions reached is entirely that of the Author, and the ICSSR bears no responsibility for them.]

PRINTED IN INDIA

Published by J.L. Kumar for Anmol Publications Pvt. Ltd., New Delhi - 110 002 and Printed at Mehra Offset Press, Delhi.

Contents

Acknowledgments

This study was carried out under the scheme of General Fellowship of the Indian Council of Social Science Research (ICSSR), New Delhi. Late Dr. K.K. Siddh, Director, ICSSR was instrumental in encouraging me to go for the fellowship. His untimely demise was personal loss to me. At the ICSSR point all concerning officials provided necessary help and cooperation. Particularly Dr. V.N. Sondhi, Asstt. Director, was always ready to extend friendly cooperation and hassle-free environment. Mr. K.L. Khera, Dy. Director was equally sympathetic. Mrs.Rachna Jain, Astt. Director, was ever helpful in sorting out various official formalities. Dr. A.P. Mangla, Dy. Director sanctioned Publication grants for bringing out this study in book form.

During the fellowship period I was affiliated to the Centre for South, Central, Southeast Asian and Southwest Pacific Studies, School of International Studies (SIS), Jawaharlal Nehru University (JNU), and was fortunate to receive cooperation from all faculties. Specifically, Prof. B.D. Arora, Prof. P.K. Das, Prof. B.D. Ghoshal and Dr. Ganganath Jha were always ready to help me out in one or the other way. Prof. G.P. Deshpande, Prof. I.N. Mukherjee and Prof. Nancy Jetley were quite considerate towards my research. Prof. V. Suryanarayan, University of Madras and Prof. P.V. Rao, Osmania University permitted me to consult rare literature available in their centre libraries.

Prof. Suresh Tendulkar, Delhi School of Economics, was a source of encouragement right from the beginning and advised me on many occasions. Prof. Pulin Nayak and Prof. Jean Dreze, Delhi School of Economics, were quite curious about the progress of research and their enquiry kept me working to take the study to logical end. Mr. Arun Kumar, former Joint Secretary and Mr. P.S. Ray, the present Joint Secretary, Policy Planning Divn. Ministry of External Affairs supported me by giving feed-back on various aspects of the study and were ever ready to discuss the research problem.

Prof. Stanley Nollen, Georgetown University, USA was ever youthful in advising me on many occasions and lent me support by discussing the research problem. During his frequent visits to New Delhi, over the past few years he exchanged his research experience and took keen interest in my research progress. Both Basu, Prof. Kaushik and Prof. Alka, Cornell University, USA were always enthusiastic about my research work and I was beneficiary of their friendly advice. Dr. Ashutosh Thakur, JNU helped me in many ways and was closely associated with this work.

During my sojourn at the Institute of New Technology, United Nations University, Maastricht, the Netherlands I got benefit of interaction with Prof. Charles Cooper, Director. Similarly, other faculties of the institute namely, Prof. Swasti Mitter, Dr. Shulin Gu, Dr. Sunil Mani and Dr. Joonghae Suh discussed the problem at length. Dr. Servass Storm, Department of Economics, Erasmus University, Rotterdam, the Netherlands helped me by supplying related literature on the subject. I would like to express my sincere gratitude towards all of them.

Preface

It is almost a decade now that India unveiled "look-east policy" in early 1992 to integrate its economy with the economies of Asia. To begin with, within Asia, India consciously selected Southeast Asia as a launching platform to revitalize economic integration. This selection was on the basis of spectacular performance of five economies of Southeast Asia namely Indonesia, Malaysia, Philippines, Singapore and Thailand in recent period. India has had an age-old trade and cultural relations with all these five countries. Obviously, on India's part "look-east policy" was not merely an attempt to revive and renew these relations but to send right signal to business community of India and Southeast Asia regarding country's earnestness in globalizing its economy.

During 1980s and 1990s the above mentioned 'five' economies of Southeast Asia were recognized world over as the economically most "vibrant" countries. Their trade and investment performance was considered as exemplary to other developing countries. Most of their economic transactions with the outside world were being carried out under the united banner of ASEAN. In 1967 the Association of Southeast Asian Nations (ASEAN) was formed by these 'five' nations to address issues relating to intensification of their mutual political relations. However, in the later period their economic concerns took precedence over political issues and the concerted efforts were made to enhance intra-regional trade and investment cooperation.

In 1983 Brunei was admitted as the sixth member and in 1994 Vietnam was enrolled as seventh member of the ASEAN. Gradually, in subsequent years, the ASEAN was expanded by admitting Laos and Mynamar and lately, i.e. in April 1999 Cambodia was taken in as a tenth and last member to culminate the entire Southeast Asia as a ASEAN region.

India being relatively 'late comer' in the ASEAN region was deprived of the early benefits of economic interaction which other countries could reap owing to their understanding of the importance of region in their future business. Nevertheless between 1992 and 1996 India demonstrated willingness by putting ASEAN region on priority list of her trade and investment transactions. The prospects of India-ASEAN relations suffered setback between 1997 and mid-1999 because of two reasons: First India was under political instability when no government at the Centre could able to survive for more than one year and in a short span of two and half years three governments were toppled down. The political uncertainty distorted the direction of economic reforms which were launched in July 1991. Second in July 1997 majority of Southeast and East Asian nations plunged into financial turmoil. The financial crisis basically emanated from some ASEAN countries and turned their economic progress topsy-turvy. India too was inflicted by the virus of crisis when her exports were adversely affected and the GDP growth rate was slowed down.

The general elections in September 1999 ended political instability in India and the new government at the Centre pledged commitment to launching of second generation economic reforms. Already the government made the ball rolling by opening insurance sector to private and foreign investors. Various liberalization and globalization related policy issues are high on present government agenda and in coming years many favourable changes may take place. Particularly improvement in physical infrastructure with the helpof private and foreign investment tops the government agenda.

After four years of the Asian crisis the Southeast ASIAN countries are gradually coming up and may pick up rapid recovery under their joint programme of 'Vision 2020'. The objective of 'Vision 2020' is to integrate all the ten ASEAN nations economically, politically and socially as single entity. India too drafted a plan of "Vision 2020" to transform the developing economy into a developed one by year 2020. To achieve this goal, the key captains of Indian government and private sector are working together to concentrate on five selected areas namely agriculture and food processing, electric power, education and health, information technology and strategic sectors.

In their attempts to achieve respective goals, both India and ASEAN can explore new possibilities to enhance their mutual economic interaction. Their coming together may give new direction to economic viability of the Asia region. Here in this study we have assessed the outcome of India-ASEAN economic partnership since 1985 by highlighting two-way trade and investment transactions between them. The discussion mainly revolves around the theme - what was the impact of "look-east policy" on India's trade and investment relations with ASEAN countries over the period. Besides, we have analysed the oft-repeated question in Indian intelligentsia—does East look at India as its economic partner.

The scheme of the book perhaps requires a word of explanation. The first chapter is a broad and fairly comprehensive introduction of the study. It highlights current developments in ASEAN and Indian economy by pointing out principal characteristics of both. The chapter second explains economic scenario in world, India and ASEAN and brings out comparative significance of India and ASEAN in global trade and investment transactions. It also takes into consideration China's position as a competitor to India in the ASEAN region. The chapter third is exclusively dedicated to Indo-ASEAN trade relations. It focuses on trade intensity of India in Asean market and *vice-versa*. It gives comprehensive picture of various aspects of trade such as commodity structure, competitive advantage, future potentials, etc. Its main thrust is on identifying India's principal competitors in ASEAN market. The Chapter fourth deals with Indo-ASEAN investment interaction and highlights India's investment policy *vis-a-vis* other competitors such as China. It also spells out future potential between India and ASEAN. The chapter fifth concerns about formulation of AFTA and its possible implications for India's trade and investment relations with ASEAN. It also covers wider debate on trade creation and trade diversion associated with regional trading arrangements. The sixth and last chapter details out various challenges before ASEAN and the role India can play in resolving them. This chapter also draws the outline of future trend in trade and investment relations between India and Asean.

The entire study has been carried out in the aftermath of Asian financial and economic crisis when barring Singapore all other ASEAN-5 countries were severely shaken by the crisis shock. Naturally ASEAN's overall economic performance and interaction with India was greatly influenced by the crisis and we have substantially dealt with this aspect. The related fall out of the crisis was that majority of ASEAN-5 countries suffered political turmoil and brought to the fore shortcomings in their political institutions. Although the focus of the study is economic interaction nevertheless we have given substantial space and consideration to politico issue too wherever it was due in discussion.

List of Tables

Annexures

Tables

Annexures

Tables

1

Introduction

The synonymous terminology for Southeast Asia is ASEAN region because all the ten countries of the region are now members of the ASEAN (regional) forum.[1] It was a long cherished dream of the ASEAN convenors to make the forum a compact organization by bringing all countries of the region under one umbrella to work together with definite and common objectives. The 'dream' has partly been fulfilled after its existence over past three decades in the sense that the forum is able to establish its image as vibrant economic entity. The four countries of the region, namely Singapore, Malaysia, Indonesia and Thailand were recognized as 'economic tigers' and were part of 'economic miracle' in Asia in 1990s. These 'four' countries' rapid economic progress during 1980s and 1990s was often cited as role model to other developing countries and the outside world was quite eager to interact with these economies.

Roughly between 1983 and 1996 the five countries of ASEAN region enjoyed high economic growth rate. Along with above mentioned 'four' countries, Philippines too performed moderately well and the group was known as ASEAN-5. The symptoms of deceleration in their economic performance were quite evident since the beginning of 1997 but no one could predict that major reverses were in store for these countries. In July 1997 the financial crisis brokeout in Thailand and subsequently engulfed the other three nations of the region namely, Indonesia, Malaysia and Philippines. Along with these four ASEAN countries, South Korea of East Asia was the fifth nation, which was hit by the crisis contagion. Almost all Asian countries (including India) came under crisis effect. Various questions were raised in many quarters of the world about the viability and sustainability of economic performance achieved by ASEAN-5 in past three decades. Some analysts were even sceptical about the rapid recovery of ASEAN-5 in coming days.

India being a business partner with ASEAN nations and linked with global economy could not prevent the entry of the (crisis) virus entering in her economy. The country came under the contagion effect as almost whole of Asia came under 'vicious effects' of financial turmoil. The crisis virus largely affected Indian financial market when large scale capital flight took place on country's stock exchange owing to massive withdrawal of investment by FIIs and domestic private investors. The virus also dampened the country's exports and industrial production and in a way adversely affected GDP growth. Nonetheless, India could able to arrest the virus spreading into wider sectors of the economy and turning it into an epidemic.

Here in this chapter we would highlight the basic points relating to ASEAN and Indian economy such as economic characteristics, trade orientation etc. in order to prepare the background for analyzing economic cooperation between them. While doing so the thrust will be on their trade and investment policies and major economic events taking place since 1985, in both the economies.

Economic Characteristics of ASEAN and India

Within the region, Singapore is an economic driving force for rest of the ASEAN nations. Notwithstanding its small size, both population and area-wise, the country is remarkably one of the important players in global economy. The 'city state' of Singapore has 3 million population with total surface area over 1000 sq. km. The predominance of service sector and absence of agriculture sector is its special feature and it is the only country in the region without prevalence of poverty. It has established the efficient service centre in the field of finance, air-lines, computer network, shipping, etc. Its production base is essentially more capital than labour intensive. The economy's "degree of openness" is 2.59 during 1992-98 which is the best among all ASEAN nations indicating that the country is much ahead in privatizing and opening.[2] The openness is reflected in hosting the large FDI amount: about US$ 7 billion annually during 1992-98. Its trade policies are outward looking with emphasis on export orientation and open import regime. On the basis of its exceptionally high per capita income (US$30060 in 1998) the Singapore can be called as developed economy [See Table : 1.1].

Indonesia is the largest economy in the ASEAN region with population about 200 million in 1998 and surface area 1905 ('000 sq. km.). The country is endowed with abundant stock of natural resources. The two sectors, industry and services, are most leading and their combined share in national income is about 70 percent in 1998. The economy although can not be called as poverty ridden but about 15 per cent of its population in 1990 was below poverty-line. The economy is moderately 'outward looking' compared to other ASEAN economies and its degree of openness is 0.47 in 1992-98 which is lowest among ASEAN-5 nations.[3]

Malaysia is best endowed with natural resources compared to other ASEAN countries. It has relatively a large and fertile land area surrounded by long coastlines. Its major export commodities are petroleum, wood, palm oil, rubber and tin. There are many similarities between Indonesia and Malaysia in the matter of availability of natural resources. However Malaysia is better placed than Indonesia on the basis of the per capita income: For Malaysia it is US$3600 and for Indonesia US$680 in 1998. Malaysia's degree of openness has risen to 1.63 in 1992-98 from 1.19 in 1985-91 suggesting that the country has further liberalized during recent period. The more openness has led to hosting of higher amount of foreign investment. The (average) annual FDI inflows in 1992-98 was US$4.6 billion. The country is outward looking and India has substantial trade interaction with Malaysia.

Philippines is third largely populated country in the region with 75 million people and the per capita income was US$1050 in 1998. The share of agriculture in national income of the economy is rapidly receding and that of service is surging ahead. At the same time the share of industry and manufacturing has almost remained unchanged between 1985 and 1998. About 38 percent of the population is below poverty-line. The degree of openness over the period has improved and the economy is reasonably attractive to host FDI to the tune of US$1.3 billion (annually) in 1992-98.

The economic performance of Thailand between 1985 and 1996 was consistently remarkable and average GDP growth rate over the period was 10 percent. The World Bank even adjudged it in 1995 as the fastest growing developing economy in the world. But surprisingly since July 1997 the world is watching the dark days for Thai economy because of much discussed financial crisis first brokeout in the country. Many critics found the roots of the crisis in unmindful opening of the economy's financial sector to the foreign investors without making provision for (counter balancing) regulatory mechanism to check growth of hot money in circulation. That apart, there were other reasons causing crisis and they are discussed in detail here at proper places.

In Thai's national income the contribution of service sector is about 50 percent and that of industry is 40 percent and significance of the agriculture sector is rapidly declining. The per capita income in 1998 was US$2200 and about 13 percent population was living below poverty line in 1992. Among ASEAN-5, Thailand had the highest export-growth rate (22 per cent) in 1985-91. However, in 1992-98 the export growth rate decreased much to 11 percent. Because of high degree of openness in 1992-98 the (average) annual FDI inflows in the economy was about US$3 billion.

Currently, Thailand, is in the process of restructuring the economy after the financial turmoil, mostly with the financial support from International Monetary Fund (IMF). The crisis has shaken almost all the sectors and challenged viability of the economy's fundamentals. Going by the ongoing trend and efforts of rebuilding, the Thai economy would require relatively long period to attain, if not full, adequate recovery.

Among the rest of five nations of ASEAN, Brunei is oil rich and substantial part of her national income comes from the exports of petroleum and oil products. Population-wise it is a tiny nation with only 0.3 million people in 1998 and having a surface area of 5800 sq.km.[4] India, of late, is trying to enhance her cooperation with Brunei but her relations are largely restricted to import of oil and petroleum products.

The other countries of ASEAN Vietnam, Laos, Myanmar and Cambodia are more or less endowed with similar sort of natural resources. These countries are relatively laggard in exploiting the resources mainly because of inadequate availability of financial and skilled human resources. Lately, Vietnam has been making stride to integrate its economy with the region's economies and outside world. The lifting of US economic embargo on Vietnam in 1993 has facilitated the economy to transact business rigorously with many countries. It is the second largest populated country (about 80 million people in 1998) in ASEAN region with 51 percent person living below poverty line.

Laos, Myanmar and Cambodia are least developed economies with strong presence of agricultural sector and less developed industry, manufacturing and services sectors. All these three countries are poverty ridden having large chunk of their population living below subsistence level. Their trade policies are inward looking implying promotion of import substitution. These economies though opening up some sectors to foreign investors lack in availability of the efficient infrastructure. The small size their domestic market is the principal obstacle in flowing in large FDI in these economies. Nevertheless, the relatively developed economies of ASEAN are intensifying their economic ties with these countries and their efforts may help to elevate these countries' economic status. India has traditional trade relations with all these three countries but two-way transactions, both volume and value wise, are restricted to low level.

In the backdrop of varied characteristics of ASEAN countries it would be interesting to evaluate India's principal economic features. Populations wise India's size is double than collective population of ASEAN region. India is a country of 1 billion persons where 40 percent population stays below poverty line. The per capita income in 1998 is US$430. The share of agriculture in national income in recent period is falling and that of industry and services is rising up. The degree of openness in 1992-98 is 0.20 which is much lower than value of ASEAN-5. The inflow of FDI in 1990s has picked up with the advent of economic reforms in July 1991 and the country could able to host FDI US$1.7 billion annually during 1992-98. The economy may not be labelled as 'export oriented' but there are efforts to wipe out the earlier image of 'import substituting' country. From the mindset of 'export pessimism' the country is moving toward 'positive exportism' by allocating prime position to all out exports.[5]

Simultaneously efforts are on to privatize public enterprises and invite foreign investors to take up projects in infrastructure and other related sectors. There is realization that unless domestic market is widely opened up for foreign consumer products the economy would not become favourable destination for large FDI doses. To do so, the general import tariffs are lowered in 1990s: from the very high of 150 percent to 50 percent in 1995 and further to between 25 and 40 percent in 1998. These rates may further be slashed to bring them at par with international level.

Moreover, quantitative restrictions on import volume are being brought down to assure larger share of domestic demand to foreign manufacturers. The perception about FDI is changing and it is seen as facilitator of rapid economic development. The FDI is now seen as substitute for external financial borrowing with comparative advantage of bringing in foreign technology.

Recent Developments in ASEAN Region and Its Imperative Impact on India–ASEAN Interaction

(a) India becoming a Dialogue Partner

India became a 'sectoral dialogue' partner with ASEAN forum in 1992. Under the arrangement of sectoral dialogue partnership four areas were earmarked for mutual cooperation between India and ASEAN, namely trade, investment, tourism and science and technology. A formal institutional linkage was established between ASEAN and India in 1993 when the sectoral dialogue relationship was inaugurated. In following two years the status of sectoral dialogue partner upgraded to 'full dialogue' partner in 1995 and India was invited to participate in ASEAN post Ministerial Conference in Jakarta in July 1996.[6] At the conference, the ASEAN and Indian Ministers outlined a vision of a shared destiny and intensified cooperation in all the fields.

In the follow up to these steps, ASEAN-India Joint Cooperation Committee (JCC) was established to function as a key institutional mechanism for providing substantive content and implementing programmes of cooperation. The first meeting of JCC was held in New Delhi in November 1996 and ASEAN India Working Group on Science and Technology and Trade and Investment were established. The JCC recognized India's expertise in the field of science & technology and agreed that further consolidation of cooperation is possible in three areas such as Advanced Materials, Bio-technology and Information technology. The other related activities where Indian expertise can be relevant to ASEAN are food processing, health, agriculture engineering, electronics, communications and services.

(b) Part of East Asian Miracle

In September 1993, the World Bank has brought out an empirical study entitled - "The East Asian Miracle: Economic Growth and Public Policy" which stirred the research environment working on East Asia region as it critically focussed the key growth-agents of the region.[7] The study highlighted the eight countries of the region as High Performing Asian Economies (HPAEs) which could achieve highest growth rates in the world between 1965 and 1990. The eight HPAEs were Japan; plus the four countries falling under the category of first-tier newly industrialising economies (NIEs) namely Hong Kong, Taiwan, Singapore and South Korea; and plus three countries falling under the category of second-tier newly industrialising countries (NICs) namely Indonesia, Malaysia and Thailand. Thus out of eight HPAEs the four belonged to ASEAN region. According to the study the superior growth record of HPAEs is to be attributed largely to their superior accumulation of physical and human capital over the period.

Besides, the study appreciated the active and considerable government intervention in respective countries in attaining the status of HPAEs. The government intervention was particularly visible in achieving equity in income distribution by way of introducing progressive income tax, welfare programmes and other measures for equity. There were following six common features which distinguished HPAEs from other countries of the region -

(i) more rapid output and productivity growth in agriculture,

(ii) higher rates of growth of manufactured exports,

(iii) earlier and steeper declines in fertility,

(iv) higher growth rates of physical capital, supported by higher rates of domestic savings,

(v) higher initial levels and growth rates of human capital, and

(vi) generally higher rates of productivity growth.

Although some of the findings of the study were well received generally but there were certain serious shortcomings, particularly concerning income distribution pattern in the ASEAN economies. The domestic income distribution in first-tier NIE of ASEAN, i.e., Singapore and second-tier NICs that is, Indonesia, Malaysia and Thailand though apparently looks equal in comparison with other developing countries, however, in reality, the situation is much far from the truth. In the aftermath of financial crisis of 1997, various flaws in income distribution in second-tier NICs has come to the fore which exposed the wide disparity in income level in their society. Moreover, there are wide income gaps among member countries of the ASEAN.[8] For instance, per capita GDP of Singapore is very much bigger than that of Laos or Cambodia or Mynamar. Such wide difference in income level and economic structure among member states may put spoke in their endeavour to achieving solidarity of ASEAN forum in future.

The same study while emphasizing the role of government intervention in achieving the status of HPAEs, especially in Japan, Taiwan, and South Korea is reluctant to approve gains from industrial policy in Southeast Asian Second-tier NICs. The study maintains that the rapid growth of Indonesia, Malaysia and Thailand is basically because of adopting the export-push strategies and courting foreign direct investment and creating a favourable environment for exporters without at the same time following policies of financial repression and industrial targeting. Thus, the study claims that these three aforesaid economies have grown rapidly by relying on market forces and minimal on industrial policy. The report advocates that the other developing countries, where similar sort of environment such as one in Southeast Asian Second-tier NICs is present, can imitate the model for their rapid economic growth.

However, a section of regional economists are critical about the World Bank's observations concerning beneficiary effect of industrial policy in Southeast Asian second-tier NICs and find it very much erroneous.[9] They maintain that the consequences of state intervention in Southeast Asian Second-tier NICs have been mixed and it is largely because much of the state intervention has been motivated by considerations other than accelerating late industrialization. However, given the limitations of second-tier NICs' market there is need of effective state intervention in the areas such as i) enhancing level of technology, ii) mobilising finance for further industrialization, iii) enhancing the productivity of human resource and ensuring appropriate training to labour force, and iv) maintaining higher level of export growth. Nevertheless these regional economists had doubted the sustainability of prosperity of second-tier NICs mainly because unlike Northeast Asian economies these economies had been heavily dependent on foreign investment. Their suspicion had somewhat proved to be true when the prosperity bubble of these economies had blown up with the eruption of financial crisis.

The sustainability of second-tier NICs was also questioned, although for other reasons. The economic growth of these NICs had been likened to a flock of 'flying geese' and the 'lead goose' was Japan. Now when Japan itself is in trouble and experiencing economic slowdown over the past several years there is possibility that this (Japan's) situation may have adverse impact on the growth of NICs.[10]

(c) Formation of AFTA

In 1992 the six nations of ASEAN region namely, Brunei, Indonesia, Malaysia, Philippines, Singapore and Thailand decided to formulate ASEAN Free Trade Area (AFTA) and since then six countries began the process of reducing tariffs to bring them in the range of 0-5 per cent on all commodities traded between them. Similarly there are efforts to remove all non-tariff barriers presently existing between these six countries. The AFTA will come into force on January 1, 2003 and initially the aforesaid six countries will implement the free trade provisions. Gradually, in the later period, the left out four countries of the region, will be accommodated under the AFTA framework.

The formation of AFTA reflects both, developments within ASEAN and the changing international economic and political environment. Internally, rapid industrialization in the 'six' ASEAN countries has given rise to greater intra-ASEAN trade, particularly in manufactured products. Trade has also become more complementary than competitive among the six ASEAN countries. Externally, the changes wrought in the international sphere have exerted pressure on ASEAN to strengthen its cooperation within the area. The emergence of regional blocks such as the Single European Market (SEM) and North American Free Trade Agreement (NAFTA) have also had a major impact on ASEANs' perception of the global trading system. Fears of trade and investment diversion, coupled with increasing competition for FDI, have forced ASEAN to forge closer economic ties among its members.

The formulation of AFTA throws open both challenges as well as opportunities to India. The challenges would be the regional trading blocs even though talks of "open regionalism" but in reality practice "close regionalism" against the principle of multilateralism. If within the trading bloc the trade becomes free between regional partners, however, with the outside region the trade becomes more and more discriminatory at bilateral level. The erection of higher tariff walls and practice of other restrictive measures such as quota, prohibit the entry of goods entering the bloc, from outside the region. Going by the behaviour of other trading blocs like NAFTA, Single European Market or MERCOSUR in Southern Cone of Latin America, there is strong possibility that AFTA may also follow the similar line up of these fellow trading blocs in the longer run.[11]

(d) Birth of APEC

The most important development in the Asia-pacific region in the recent period is the formation of Asia-Pacific Economic Cooperation (APEC) in 1989. The APEC became operational in 1996 following Subic Bay Summit. Initially the APEC was a group of 18 countries, namely Brunei, Indonesia, Malaysia, Philippines, Singapore, Thailand, USA, Canada, Mexico, Australia, Newzealand, Papua New Guinea, China, Hong Kong, Taiwan, South Korea, Japan and Chile. In the fifth APEC summit in 1998, the group was expended by admitting Vietnam, Peru, and Russia. Presently, there is moratorium on the expansion of APEC membership otherwise since its formation India made several attempts to get inducted into the forum. The APEC is seen as an 'enlarged shadow' of ASEAN in the region which is a combination of developed and developing nations. About 42 percent of world's total trade is transacted among the members countries.[12]

The APEC has an ambitious agenda of building a regional community and abolishing trade and investment barriers. Recently, it has unveiled a plan of achieving free and open trade and investment by year 2010 (for developed countries) and year 2020 (for developing countries) of APEC. Its agenda is not constrained merely to liberalization of trade and investment but facilitation of trade, investment, economic, and technical cooperation within APEC region. The forum also covers an unusually wide range of issues including services and investment.[13]

(e) Outbreak of Asian Crisis

In the early hours of July 2, 1997, the Bank of Thailand announced it was letting the baht (i.e. Thai Currency) float. The currency went into free-fall, triggering a currency crisis in the region, then a financial crisis, then a full-fledged economic meltdown. This was followed by political tumult in some countries of the region. Southeast Asia's economic turmoil has convulsed the region's political institutions, exposing their major fault lines and throwing the region into its deepest period of instability in a generation.[14]

The worst affected economies from financial crisis were Thailand, Indonesia. Malaysia, Philippines and South Korea. With the exception of Malaysia, the remaining four were forced to visit International Monetary Fund (IMF) due to their overblown short-term debts and current account deficits in relation to their international reserves.

The crisis, in general, was the result of a combination of various factors weak economic fundamentals because of overheating of the currencies plus poorly supervised liberalization in the above mentioned four ASEAN economies. Although first order fundamentals such as unemployment rates, inflation, savings and GDP growth rates were substantially satisfactory, however the critical variables such as the current account imbalances and soaring private credit affected Indonesia, Malaysia, Philippines and Thailand. Investment rates involving these four economies continued to exceed GDP growth rates, reflecting little productivity growth and suggesting slow technological progress.[15] Even much before occurring of the crisis the doubts were expressed about the longevity of prosperity and its sustainability in these four countries. The suspicion were mainly about the fundamental of these economies as there was little evidence of improvement in the efficiency, in terms of labour and technology. The prosperity mainly centred around private property boom in real estate and that too mostly relying on private borrowings from abroad.[16]

For each of these four ASEAN economies the causes of the crisis and its impacts were varying and it would be imperative to look into details to understand the problem.

Thailand

Basically, the financial crisis in Thailand was due to excessive investments. During the 1990-96 period the investment ratio (i.e. gross domestic investment as a percentage of GDP) was between 40 per cent and 44 per cent, compared to average investment ratios of 25 per cent and 30 per cent during the 1980-84 and 1985-89 periods respectively. Many investments were based on money borrowed from abroad. Due to high interest rates in Thailand and a fixed exchange rate policy, i.e., linking baht to the US dollar, foreign investors were eager to place their money in Thailand, preferring to lend on a short-term basis (for three or six months).

In 1992, as a part of a broader financial liberalization package, the government deregulated the foreign exchange. As a consequence, Thailand undertook too much offshore borrowings. The external debt increased from almost US$ 40 billion in 1992 to US $80 billion in March 1997. Thus, total outstanding debt as a share of GDP increased from 34 per cent in 1990 to 51 per cent in 1996 and this increase generated almost exclusively by the private sector. Further the ratio of short-term debt to foreign reserves increased from 0.6 in 1990 to 1.0 in 1995 and 1996, implying that the ability of the country to service short-term debt had deteriorated during the first half of 1990s.

The massive inflow of money tripled the amount of loans in the financial system, causing misallocation of investment resources. An investment bubble was thus created by careless lending. A substantial part of the money was channeled into already inflated assets in the real estate sector. Many property owners artificially inflated the value of their assets and kept borrowing against them, while most real companies had poor cash flows.[17]

Thus Thai economy between 1990 and 1996 experienced boom-bust cycle involving property and stock markets. When the economic recession started in 1996 and buying power of the middle and upper classes began declining, the property bubble burst and left substantial bad debts on the balance sheet of the finance companies, which had financed their investments by borrowing abroad.

During 1996, it became clear that the Thai economy had lost its momentum. The economy was slowing down to the lowest rate of GDP growth in a decade. Thailand suddenly experienced negative export growth and export sales of labour-intensive goods. As imports kept growing, the current account deficit increased. Meanwhile, the stock exchange lost around one fifth of its value during the first nine months of 1996, implying a stock market collapse prior to the currency crisis. Between 1994 and 1996, the current account deficit was ballooning at an average of 40 per cent every six months. As the share of GDP, the current account deficit reached 8 per cent in 1996.

Given the deteriorating situation of the Thai economy the currency traders made some preliminary attacks on the baht in November-December 1996. The currency crisis hit Thailand in early March 1997 after a speculative on the baht in February 1997 had driven up inter-bank rates and made liquidity tighter. Speculators realised that the Thai currency was overvalued and that speculative attacks would lead to a lowering of the baht's value. Looking at the precarious situation, some local investors began selling baht for US dollars in order to hedge against a possible devaluation, while exporters increasingly delayed converting their export earnings into baht. As a consequence, there was a huge supply of baht in money market. In May 1997, with severe problems in the financial sector unsolved and with no sign of economic recovery, a new series of attacks on the baht took place.

During the first quarter of 1997, the property bubble burst. The real-estate companies and property companies had difficulty in servicing their debts. By late July 1997 the investors' confidence of baht and financial sector broke down and the baht became unstable and volatile. The Bank of Thailand (BOT) no longer seen as a safety net for the leading financial institutions and confidence in the BOT itself had fallen.

At this juncture the FIIs started withdrawing their investment from the country thinking that the value of baht may worsen in short period. The investors of the region took panicky decisions and fund managers based outside the region, for example, in Wall Street or the city of London-behaved in "herd like" fashion, causing a "contagion" or "domino" effect throughout the region. The large scale funds from the various stock markets of ASEAN region were withdrawn in a short period. The Thai crisis unraveled an unusual phenomenon, that is, financial markets are driven not by only "fundamentals" but "sentiments" too.

Indonesia

The contagion effect of Thai crisis struck Indonesia in few hours of baht devaluation in July 1997. The Indonesian economy found itself in a state of near collapse in January 1998. Between a period of July 1997 and January 1998 the Indonesian economy witnessed large scale investment withdrawal. Indonesia basically hit by crisis because of excessive expansion and weak banking system which was a result of imprudent financial liberalization the country had undertaken since the 1980s.

With the eruption of crisis, Indonesia resorted to adjustment policies of tight credit and higher interest rates that exacerbated the weakness in the banking system. The purpose of credit constriction was to reduce expected profits in private companies (particularly in real sectors), and the banking system. These abetted further attacks on the equity and asset markets, worsening the performance of the country's currency, i.e. rupiah. The worsening rupiah further weakened the economy's prospects and encouraged investment withdrawal.[18]

Malaysia

Since mid-July 1997, the Malaysian currency - ringgit (RM) has fallen precipitously, reaching RM 4.88 to the US dollar in January 1998, its lowest level ever. The collapse was by almost half within half a year from a high of RM 2.47 in July 1997. Besides (ringgit depreciation), the

Malaysian stock markets were collapsed more severely. Among various causes of the economy collapse, the principal was too much presence of 'short-term' investments in non-tradables, such as construction and real property. Such short-term investments - involving loans with collateral, worsened the current account trade deficits. According to the Bank of International Settlements (BIS), 56 per cent of foreign borrowings, in January 1998 from commercial banks were short-term in nature.[19]

Philippines

Even earlier in 1980s the Philippines has suffered a foreign debt crisis similar to Latin America. The July 1997 financial crisis can be broadly linked to "crony capitalism" and mismanagement of the economy during the crisis period. Right from the beginning of the year 1997 the slowing down of the economy was clearly visible. The economy had experienced high growth rate between 1990 and 1996 mostly owing to opening of the economy. The opening on the front of foreign exchange and capital account led to increases in net foreign investments. The remittances of overseas Filipino workers also led to increase in foreign investments. Capital liberalization led to massive portfolio inflows and outflows that increased volatility on external account as short-run money (i.e. hot money) came in and turned around very quickly.

The net external inflows of capital led to appreciation of the 'peso', the Philippines currency, in real terms. The currency appreciation hurt the export sector and in conjunction with significant tariff reluction, increased tremendously the import intensity of the economy. This bias against tradables encouraged the fast-growing economy to shift to non-tradables, particularly, the real property, finance and trade sectors. This, together with the overloading syndrome in the finance sector, created asset bubbles. The financial liberalization and easing of bank entry allowed the overgrowing and overlending syndrome to unfold in full force without sufficient prudential regulation by the Central Bank.[20]

The overall decline of growth rates for the first and second quarters of 1997 was further joined by slowing down of export growth rate. The slower growth rate had an impact on stock market which went down to unprecedented depth. The devaluation of-Thai baht had an adverse effect on foreign investments and with the spurt of crisis in neighbouring economies, the portfolio inflows suddenly left Philippines.

Thus to summarise, the principal causes of crises were: there was liberalization of domestic financial systems without applying prudential norms to check excessive foreign borrowings from commercial banks which was essentially short-term in nature and mostly invested in non-tradable sector; besides opening of capital account for all purpose. The liberalization of the capital account has essentially guaranteed non-residents ease of exit as well as fewer limitations on nationals holding foreign assets and thus inadvertently facilitating capital flight. Further, removing controls on capital inflows effectively subsidised net outflows. Opening the capital account has also provided foreign fund managers with access to domestic bond and stock markets, and given the domestic financial systems access to lower cost funds from abroad.[21]

The crisis is of special concern to India as the country's stock exchange experienced heavy withdrawal of investment by FIIs during the turmoil period. The crisis has raised many doubts about wide opening of financial sector. There has been a demand to make Indian rupee fully convertible on capital account but the government is reluctant to accept it taking into consideration the ill effects of full convertibility in ASEAN-5 countries. The availability of full convertibility on capital account in ASEAN-5 tempted and facilitated FIIs to withdraw their investments.[22]

Another important lesson India can draw from the crisis is that mere rise in exports for a sufficiently long period is no assurance of sustainability of foreign exchange reserves. All the ASEAN-5, until crisis struck to their economies, were enjoying fairly large surplus balance on their foreign reserves owing to high export growth rate. But once the stock market started crashing the concerned governments failed to stop depreciation of their currencies and flight of foreign exchange. What is essential is to hold the confidence of the shareholders by adopting pro-active role by government and quick intermediation in financial market at the time of crisis.[23] The Indian financial markets over the period are deepened greatly with good proportion of money supply (M2) to GDP because of growth of very large equity and bond markets (including a large private bond market) and this has greatly increased the liquidity of the financial system. Thus presently the fundamentals of the Indian economy are satisfactory and the government is deploying measures to make it fail-safe in future.[24]

(f) Formulation of ASEAN Investment Area

In the light of financial crisis in the region the ASEAN Heads of Investment Agencies (AHIA), met in July 1998 in Singapore to strengthen regional cooperation in promoting greater direct investment into and within the region. The AHIA noted that FDI and intra-ASEAN investment flows have declined dramatically since the beginning of the crisis and felt that there is need to take collective action and measures in addition to those taken in the individual member countries. The AHIA finalized the Framework Agreement to create ASEAN Investment Area (AIA) by 1998. The objective of the AIA is to attract greater and sustainable levels of FDI into the region from ASEAN and non-ASEAN sources. This is to be achieved by enhancing the competitiveness and attractiveness of the region's investment environment through implementing three pillars of broad based programmes. These are Cooperation and Facilitation; Promotion and Awareness; and Liberalization Programme.[25] Under the AIA agenda, it has been decided to facilitate intra-ASEAN sourcing of technology, enhancement of investment matchmaking, promotion of joint ventures operations, and to provide opportunities to technology suppliers in the region to supply technology to third countries.

(g) ASEAN Vision of 2020

Despite financial turbulence in the region, the member states are high in spirit to achieve the goal of ASEAN Economic Region by year 2020. The 'Vision 2020' underlines a creation of stable, prosperous and highly competitive ASEAN Economic Region in which there will be free flow of goods, services and investments, a freer flow of capital, equitable economic development and reduced poverty and socio-economic disparities. The 'Vision 2020' visualises an outward-looking ASEAN playing a pivotal role in the international fora. It also implies ASEANs' intensified relationship with its 'dialogue partners' and other regional organizations based on equal partnership and mutual respect.

Envisaging a prosperous ASEAN is based on certain landmark achievements of the region over the past three decades. The first and foremost is there has been no war amongst any two ASEAN in the last thirty years; so also there has been a very low probability of war between any two ASEAN states in future. The 'no war' environment has helped the region to consolidate the economic interaction between member states and strengthen economic unity within the region. The member states on the basis of region's good performance could increase their economic transactions outside the region's border. Secondly, the formation of ASEAN forum has delivered the prosperity in the region. In 1967, ASEAN's overall trade was worth US $10 billion and in 1998 it reached US $ 622 billion. It means the total ASEAN trade over the last three decades has increased by about 62 times while its population has only doubled. ASEAN is the fourth largest trading community in the world.

Over the years ASEAN forum could succeed in creation of incipient sense of community within the region. The regular, formal and informal, meetings of government executives of the member states have enabled the region to build a strong community. For instance, ASEAN generates over 300 meetings amongst senior government officials per year. Such official linkages are also complemented by non-governmental contacts.[26]

Conclusion

The ASEAN region since 1985 is full of dramatic and significant events. Despite reverses caused by financial crisis the ASEAN-5 are determined to usher in full-form and regain their pre-crisis economic vitality. There is realization about errors and wrongs committed by them in the heat of liberalization and globalization. Now these countries are in the process of restructuring their economies and corrective measures are being applied to strengthen the fundamentals of economic institutions. In these attempts, they are moving unitedly as single entity by understanding the problems of each member state.

Temporarily, trade and investment transactions of ASEAN-5 are slowed down in the aftermath of crisis and these countries will need atleast two more years to pick up earlier height. Keeping in view the present precarious situation in the region India can not expect watershed bilateral transactions with ASEAN-5 countries in next two years. Nevertheless India meanwhile need to pursue the present level of relations with these economies. Besides, India need not neglect the significance of other countries of the region namely, Vietnam, Laos, Myanmar and Cambodia given their inclusion in ASEAN forum in 1990s.

The best option open to India now is to cultivate close linkage with some influential members of APEC forum such as Australia, USA, Singapore and Japan. Because, in future, APEC will outsmart all other regional blocs on the basis of presence of strong members in the forum. Getting the membership of APEC, whenever opportunity arises in future, will ensure enhanced significance of India in global economy.[27] For time being, India needs to follow the policy of 'smooth going' with ASEAN countries to achieve long term goals.

Table 1.1

India and ASEAN : Various Basic Indicators, 1985, 1998

		India	ASEAN Total	Indonesia	Phillippines	Malaysia	Singapore	Thailand	Vietnam	Brunei	Laos	Mynamar	Cambodia
		1	2	3	4	5	6	7	8	9	10	11	12
1. Surface Area ('000 sq. Km)	1996	3288	4482	1905	300	330	1	513	332	5.8	237	677	181
2. Population (millions)	1998	980	503	204	75	22	3	61	78	0.3	5	44	11
Average annual growth (%)	1980-90	3.5	3.8	3.2	4.4	4.8	3.3	2.7	3.7	N.A.	4.4	2.7	5.0
	1990-98	2.0	2.3	1.9	2.6	2.8	2.2	1.4	2.3	N.A.	3.0	1.3	3.1
3. GNP at Market Price (US$ billion)	1998	421.3	557	138.5	78.9	79.8	95.1	134.4	25.6	N.A.	1.6	N.A.	3.0
GNP per Capita (US$)	1998	430.0		680.0	1050	3600	30060	2200	330	N.A.	330	N.A.	280
GDP(US $ million)	1985-91	221421		90332	38577	35946	25935	61333	N.A.	N.A.	745	N.A.	N.A.
Annual Average	1992-98	308109		167989	68486	77335	72594	147604	20233	N.A.	1598	N.A.	3025
4. Distribution of GDP (%)													
Agriculture	1985	31		24	27	N.A.	1	17	N.A.	N.A.	N.A.	48	N.A.
	1998	25		16	17	12	0	11	26	N.A.	52	59	51
Industry	1985	27		36	32	N.A.	37	30	N.A.	N.A.	N.A.	13	N.A.
	1998	30		43	32	48	35	40	31	N.A.	21	10	15

Contd. ...

(Table 1.1 Contd.)

		India	ASEAN Total	Indonesia	Phillippines	Malaysia	Singapore	Thailand	Vietnam	Brunei	Laos	Mynamar	Cambodia
		1	2	3	4	5	6	7	8	9	10	11	12
Manufacturing	1985	17		14	25	N.A.	24	20	N.A.	N.A.	N.A.	10	N.A.
	1998	19		26	22	34	24	29	N.A.	N.A.	16	7	06
Services	1985	41		41	41	N.A.	62	53	N.A.	N.A.	N.A.	39	N.A.
	1998	45		41	52	40	65	49	43	N.A.	27	31	34
5. Poverty (National Poverty lines) Population below the poverty line (%) year	1994	35		15.1	37.5	15.5	0	13.1	50.9	N.A.	46.1	N.A.	36.1
6. Degree of	1985-1991	0.14		0.41	0.41	1.19	3.17	0.62	N.A.	N.A.	0.21	N.A.	N.A.
openness		0.14		0.41	0.41	1.19	3.17	0.62	N.A.	N.A.	0.21	N.A.	N.A.
	1992-1998	0.20		0.47	0.71	1.68	2.89	0.72	0.66	N.A.	0.50	N.A.	0.57
7. Merchandise Trade Exports Average annual growth (%)	1985-91	10	12.4	05	08	12	15	22	27	- 2	44	15	54
	1992-98	12	13.2	09	20	14	12	11	55	-3	41	14	87

Contd. ...

(Table 1.1 Contd.)

		India	ASEAN Total	Indonesia	Phillippines	Malaysia	Singapore	Thailand	Vietnam	Brunei	Laos	Mynamar	Cambodia
		1	2	3	4	5	6	7	8	9	10	11	12
Imports Average annual growth (%)	1985-91	06	14.8	11	11	16	14	22	40	14	24	30	105
	1992-98	12	10.2	04	23	11	8	5	27	21	16	16	169
8. Foreign Direct Investment-Inflows Annual average (US $ million)	1986-91	177	7908	746	501	1605	3592	1325	68	N.A.	03	68	N.A.
	1992-98	1676	20694	2964	1282	4595	7119	2887	1522	07	69	113	135

Note:
1. Poverty Survey year for Indonesia is 1990; Philippines 1997; Malaysia 1989; Thailand 1992; Vietnam 1993; Laos 1993; Cambodia 1997.
2. In case of Laos GDP figures for the years 1985 & 86 are not available and hence annual average amount is based on figures for 1987 to 1991.
3. For the year 1996 the figures are GNP as GDP figures are not available for this year. The source for GNP figures is 'Global Development Finance and the Developing countries', published by World Bank, 1997.
4. The percentages for column 2 for Merchandise Trade are only for Asean-5.

Source: World Bank 'World Development Report', relevant years Washington DC, USA.

NOTES & REFERENCES

1. For more details about formulation of ASEAN region see preface of this study.
2. The degree of openness is the (average) ratio of the sum of exports and imports to GDP.
3. Here in this study we would give more stress on ASEAN-5 countries, namely Indonesia, Malaysia, Philippines, Singapore and Thailand basically because for these countries consistent statistical data and information is available.
4. About Burnei, hardly any statistical or economic information is available in India and therefore our interpretation is constrained to few remarks.
5. Jalan, Bimal (1997) *India's Economic Policy-Preparing for 21st Century,* Penguin, New Delhi, pp. 91-106
6. The other full Dialogue partners are Australia, Canada, China, European Union (EU), S. Korea, Newzealand, the Russian Federation, USA, United Nations Development Programme (UNDP). Pakistan is sectoral dialogue partner.
7. World Bank (1993), *The East Asian Miracle: Economic Growth and Public Policy*, Oxford University Press, New York, USA.
8. Yamashita, Shochi (1998), "ASEAN Thirty Years on: Challenges and Problems to be solved" in *ASEAN: Today and Tomorrow*, National Political Publishing House, Hanoi, Vietnam.
9. Jomo, K.S. et al. (1997), *Southeast Asia's Misunderstood Miracle: Industrial Policy and Economic Development in Thailand, Malaysia and Indonesia*, Westview Press, USA.
10. Gough, Leo (1998), *Asia Meltdown: The end of the Miracle?*, Capstone Publishing Limited, U.K.
11. More details about AFTA and its implications for India's trade and investment is in Chapter 5 of this study.
12. Ambatkar, Sanjay (1996) "Introduction" in *India and ASEAN: Economic Partnership in the 1990s and Future Prospects,* Ambatkar, et al (edt.) Gyan Publishing House, New Delhi, pp.13-18.
13. Petri, Peter A. (1997) "Measuring and Comparing Progress in APEC," in *ASEAN Economic Bulletin*, Singapore, vol. 14, No.1, pp.1-13.
14. Keenan, Faith (1998) (ed.), *'The Aftershock—How an Economic Earth-Quake is Rattling Southeast Asian Politics'*, Review Publishing Company Ltd., Hong Kong.
15. Rasiah, Rajah (2000), "The Asian Financial Crisis and Recovery Plans" in *'Southeast Asia Into the 21st Century: Crisis and Beyond'*

- A.R. Embong and J. Rudolph (ed.), Penerbit University Kabangsaan Malaysia, Bangi, Malaysia.

16. Krugman, Paul (1995), "The Myth of Asia's Miracle" in *Foreign Affairs*, 6 (73), pp. 62-78.

17. Lauridsen, Laurids S. (1998), "Thailand: Causes, Conduct, Consequences" in *Tigers in Trouble - Financial Governance, Liberalization and Crises in East Asia*, Jomo, K.S. (ed.), Zed Books. Ltd., U.K.

18. Montes, Manuel and M.A. Abdusalamov (1998), "Financial Crisis in Indonesia" in *Tigers in Trouble - Financial Governance, Liberalization and Crisis in East Asia*, Jomo, K.S. (ed.), Zed Books Ltd., U.K.

19. Jomo, K.S. (1998), "Malaysia: From Miracle to Debacle" in *Tigers in Trouble - Financial Governance, Liberalization and Crisis in East Asia*, Jomo, K.S. (ed.), Zed Books Ltd., UK.

20. Lim, Joseph Y. (1998), "The Philippines and the East Asian Economic Turmoil" in *'Tigers in Trouble - Financial Governance, Liberalization and crisis in East Asia'* Jomo, K.S. (ed.), Zed Bookd, Ltd., U.K.

21. Montes, Manuel (1998), *'The Currency Crisis in Southeast Asia,* Institute of Southeast Asian Studies, Singapore.

22. Rakshit, Mihir (1997), "Crisis, Contagion and Crash: Asian Currency Turmoil" in *ICRA Bulletin: Money & Finance* , New Delhi, No. 4, pp. 8-45.

23. Rakshit, Mihir (1998), "Retracting the Roots of Asian Troubles 1996-97, Some analytical issues and Empirical Evidence", in *ICRA Bulletin: Money & Finance*, New Delhi No.5, p.p. 7-41.

24(a).Reddy, Y.V. (1998), 'Asian Crisis: Asking the Right Questions', lecture delivered at India International Centre, New Delhi, on May 1, 1998.

(b) Stiglitz, Joseph, 'The East Asia Crisis and its Implications for India' lecture delivered at Industrial Finance Corporation of India, New Delhi, on May 19, 1998.

25. ASEAN Secretariat World Wide Website<http://www asean.

26. Mahbubani, Kishore (1998), "ASEAN Towards 2020: Strategic Goals and Critical Pathways" in *'ASEAN Towards 2020: Strategic Goals and Future Directions'* Stephen Leong (ed.), ASEAN Academic Press Ltd., London, U.K.

27. Rao, Bhanoji, V.V. (1996), "APEC and India: Emerging linkages," in Ambatkar, et., al. (edt.) *Ibid.*, pp. 219-245.

2

Economic Scenario with Perspective on Trade and Investment: World, India and ASEAN

Before we begin to analyse dimensions of economic cooperation between India and ASEAN it would be essential to see what trend is prevalent world over concerning trade and investment and its relevance to interaction between India and ASEAN. This enquiry is also imperative because no two countries can interact in isolation when the process of globalisation sweeping the world, particularly in the matter of trade and investment. Both trade and investment, are so intertwined and globalized these days that bilateral transactions between two countries come under the influence of overall world trend.

Here in this chapter we propose to highlight (i) major changes taking place in world trade and investment environment since 1985 and its impact on India and ASEAN; (ii) overall economic performance of India and ASEAN and its effect on their trade and investment; and (iii) emerging trend in trade and investment at world level and its implications for India and ASEAN.

World Economic Scenario

The world GDP growth rate in 1990-95 decelerated to 1.9 per cent from respectable high of 3.2 per cent in 1985-90.

For a brief period of 1996 and 1997 the growth rate was accelerated to 3.3 per cent but again dipped to 2 per cent in 1998 and 1999. The developing countries' GDP growth rate in 1990 and onwards was better than industrialized (developed) countries. The dismal performance of developed economies was mainly owing to stagnancy in two prominent economies, Japan and European Union (EU) for substantially long period. The growth rate of developing Asia in 1985-90 was 4.4. per cent and in 1990-97 it increased to 6.5 per cent. However, it suffered massive set-back in the next two years, i.e. 1998 and 1999 owing to Asian financial turmoil [see Table : 2.1].

On trade front, the world exports during 1985-90 and 1990-95 registered 6 per cent growth rate. But in next two years, i.e. 1997 and 1998 the exports moved in erratic fashion: first rose to 10.5 per cent and then in next year dropped to 3.5 per cent. Between 1985 and 1997 the export growth rate of developing countries was far better than developed countries. The developing Asia accounted a considerably high export growth rate [see Table : 2.2].

In case of world FDI inflows it has been observed that, in recent period, it is on tremendous upward trend. For instance, the (average) annual FDI inflows in 1992-98 has risen to US$345 billion from US$159 billion in 1986-91. However, unlike trade the share of developing economies in these inflows is relatively much less if seen against developed economies. The foreign investors normally prefer such destinations where locational advantages in terms of physical and human infrastructures are abundantly available without hassles. Another driving force for FDI is extending production base for indigenous industries of home to host countries with the purpose of manufacturing products at competitive cost. These days the large transnational corporations (TNCs) are providing momentum in accelerating FDI in the world. The TNCs normally go for acquiring equity by adopting cross-border mergers and acquisitions (M&As) of firms and as such these transactions involve large amount of foreign investment. This trend of M&As is more prevalent in developed countries and therefore these countries are capable of piling up huge stock of foreign investment [see Table : 2.3].

Regarding ongoing trend of world FDI outflows, the share of developing countries in world total amount is rapidly moving up. And this is a welcome change in the sense that bilateral investment interaction between developing countries may get momentum. The (average) annual FDI outflows of developing countries has gone up to US$47 billion in 1992-98 from US$11 billion in 1986-91. Of course, China's share in total FDI outflows of developing countries is speedily rising but its destination is mostly her satellite nations such as Taiwan and Hong Kong [see Table : 2.4].

India's Economic Scenario

Until July 1991 India had an image of 'import substituting' economy mainly because Indian market was open to only few essential foreign items. The thrust of the economic policy was to produce goods locally with indiginous technology. The argument in support of this policy was that indigenous industry could not compete with outside industry and thus there was need to pursue 'infant industry' policy for protecting domestic industry. In the absence of open door policy the Indian economy could not attract sizeable FDI in the country. The FDI inflows are incrementally related with the trade policy of host country. The more open trade regime of the economy the higher would be doses of the FDI inflows. The FDI inflows were there but its size was so small that it was hardly visible at any point of time. The end result of these orthodox policies was that the country's balance of payments continued to grapple with adverse situation, i.e. imports exceptionally higher than exports, and rising current account deficit. To correct the adverse position, the economy relied on external borrowings of financial resources in the form of debts. These practices mounted tremendous pressure on economy's foreign exchange reserves and there was fear that it would fall into debt trap in 1989-90.

To come out of this extremely precarious situation the government decided to go for widespread economic reforms to liberalize and globalize the economy. The reforms have been put into practice since July 1991 and the government announced massive devaluation of the Indian rupee to make country's exports price competitive in the international market and thereby enhance the exports earnings which was necessary to increase the reserves of foreign exchange. The economy accrued the benefits of reforms in two ways: first the country's image of 'import substituting' economy changed into 'export promoting' economy and a follower of 'openness' policy; and second foreign investors started coming in the economy with the hope that returns on their investment will increase as the country move towards higher path of globalization.[1]

The implementation of reforms reflected in overall improvement of growth rate of the economy. The GDP growth rate which used to hover around 3.5 to 4.5 per cent in 1980s jumped to 7.8 per cent in 1996. Between 1992 and 1996 the average GDP growth rate was 6.5 per cent and in the subsequent three years it descended to 5.5 per cent because of two reasons: first the virus of Asian crisis hit the economy badly and slowed down the high export growth which the country enjoyed during 1992-96. The share of export in the national income reduced to great extent between 1997 and 1999. Second the political instability during the same period made the government indecisive on economic policy front and the process of economic reforms stagnated.

Since September 1999 the economy is looking up and the GDP growth rate may touch 6.5 per cent in coming years. There are estimates about the better performance of exports and FDI inflows. The inflation rate during 1999 stayed below

3 per cent and industry and manufacturing sectors are moving upward. The government is rapidly bringing in necessary changes to implement the second generation economic reforms and the economy is experiencing overall buoyancy signaling that it would progress well in coming days.

At this juncture it needs to see how India matters in world's exports and foreign investments. This exercise is necessary because India's interaction with ASEAN countries depends upon how the country stands in world vis-à-vis ASEAN. While doing so we would bring in 'China factor' in discussion mainly because for ASEAN countries' China is a competitor vis-à-vis India, in the matter of trade and investment. The analysis would bring out ASEANs' comparative economic interest in India and China and would help India to chalk out future strategy of economic cooperation.

India's overall annual exports increased to US$28 billion in 1992-98 from US$13 billion in 1985-91.[1] In terms of share in world exports it is 0.6 per cent and 0.5 per cent in the same period. On the contrary, China's overall exports has gone up to US$133 billion from US$48 billion over the same period. Again China's share in world exports is 3 per cent and 2 per cent during same period. China is much ahead in exports and matters much more in world trade while India is quite laggard and needs to do lot in improving her position.

China's annual exports to ASEAN-5 in 1992-98 has gone up to US$9160 million from US $3692 million in 1985-91. Similarly her annual imports from ASEAN-5 has risen to US$7824 million from US$2171 million during the same period. India's exports to ASEAN-5 during the same period has increased to US$2163 million from US$ 521 million; and her imports gone up to US$2562 million from US$1006 million. This data reveals that for the entire period (i.e. 1985 to 1998) China enjoys surplus trade balance with ASEAN-5 whereas

India accrues deficit on trade balance with ASEAN-5. China has strong trade presence in ASEAN-5 nations and India will continue to face stiff competition from China in future.

China will also compete with India in attracting FDI from the world and ASEAN-5. For the past ten years China is topping the list of developing countries in hosting FDI in the world. For instance, the annual FDI inflows in China during 1992-98 is US$34 billion, i.e. about 10 per cent share in total world FDI inflows. While India during the same period could attract US$1.7 billion (annually), i.e. about 0.5 per cent share in total world FDI inflows. India is way behind China in attracting FDI. There are many plus points in favour of China in attracting FDI. The most important is China promotes overseas ethnic Chinese to invest in China and thus about 70 per cent of her FDI comes from these people. In ASEAN countries large ethnic Chinese community is settled and they prefer to invest in China. Secondly majority of investment flows in China comes from Taiwan and Hong Kong which are 'extended territory' of mainland China. Moreover, now Hong Kong has become part of mainland China under 'one nation two systems' formula, which is an added benefit to China.

China has another advantage in interacting with ASEAN on the basis of her higher amount of FDI outflows. In 1992-98 China's annual FDI outflows in the world has gone up to US$2.7 billion from US$745 million in 1986-91. In real terms, the share in world FDI outflows has risen to 0.72 per cent from 0.41 per cent during the same period. Compared with China, the FDI outflows figures of India are absolutely negligible: US$85 million in 1992-98 and US$03 million in 1986-91. India's share in world FDI outflows during the same period is 0.02 per cent and 0.002 per cent. Thus being a low exporter of FDI, India can have lesser investment interaction with ASEAN in the sense that India can expect investment from ASEAN but not other way round. Obviously, in such situation China could become natural choice for ASEAN countries to park their investment and expect investment from China, as well. This should be taken as a pointer to India.

ASEAN-5 Economic Scenario

Between 1985 and 1996 ASEAN-5 enjoyed high economic performance mainly on the basis of being highly export oriented and investment friendly. But the same countries suffered worst in the event of Asian crisis. Even the 'miracle' economy Singapore suffered badly and its (average) annual GDP growth rate in 1998 and 1999 touched to all time low, 1.5 per cent and 0.7 per cent, respectively, which in the pre-crisis period, i.e. 1990-95 was as high as 8.5 per cent. The remaining ASEAN-4 countries experienced negative growth rate during 1998 and 1999 and it was – 9.0 and – 0.7 per cent, respectively, a dramatic fall from 7.0 per cent during 1990-95.

True to their reputation being 'outward looking', ASEAN-5 achieved an annual export growth rate of 13.2 per cent in 1992-98, a marginal rise from 12.4 per cent in 1985-91. The import growth rate, however decelerated to 10.2 per cent in 1992-98 from 14.8 per cent in 1985-91. The fall in imports is the result of financial crisis making their imports expensive in the event of depreciation of value in their currencies. Similarly, rise in exports is owing to increase in price competitiveness of their products because of drop in value of their currencies.

But that apart, ASEAN-5 has been maintaining, persistently, high export growth rate over the period, on the basis of price and quality competitiveness. ASEAN-5 share in each, world exports and imports rose to 6 per cent in 1992-98 from 4 per cent in 1985-91. This share is quite remarkable if it is compared with India.

Equally noteworthy is ASEAN-5 share in world FDI inflows: it is 6 per cent in 1992-98 and in value terms the annual FDI inflows in the same period is US$ 21 billion.

What is important from India's view point is that ASEAN-5 share in world FDI outflows in 1992-98 is US$8billion, about 2 per cent share in world total. However, it is doubtful whether ASEAN-5 could maintain the higher FDI outflows in coming days, say in next 3 years, given the bad shape of their economies in post-crisis period. It could be possible that their intra-region investment business may go up but the ASEAN investors may not attempt to opt for risk outside the region. Within the region investors may have good understanding about each others' interest in the backdrop of the crisis and therefore for the next few years the investors would opt for 'safe playing' partners.

Emerging Trend

The dip in world economic growth in recent years, i.e. 1998 and 1999 may continue in next few years because of two reasons : first the industrialized countries such as Japan and EU are not showing signs of 'looking up' from the persistent recession over the past few years and second the developing Asia would need more time to recover completely from the Asian crisis. This typical situation would call for more protectionist measures on the part of developed countries to restrict the entry of developing countries' product entering freely in their markets. The intention of developed countries were clearly manifested in recently concluded WTO trade negotiations at Seattle, USA, in November 1999. The developed countries, under the pretext of one or other reasons, like human rights, labour standards, environmental norms etc. mounted pressure on the exports of developing countries in order to safeguard their economic interest.

In both the circumstances, i.e. recessionary trend in Japan and EU and trade restrictive practices of developed countries, the developing countries need to find out ways to steer their exports in world market. One possibility, according to Dr. Joseph Stiglitz, Chief economist at World Bank, is that Asian developing countries should create internal market within Asia for their products. Over the past two decades the Asian developing countries were export oriented towards US and EU but these developed market have now reached to the point of saturation where exports of developing countries may face many problems. And thus the real growth of Asia will come from the huge internal demand existing in Asian region.[2]

Within Asia, India and China are too big markets and if ASEAN region joins with these two markets then it could become a market of about 2.5 billion people. If these 'three' apply collective policies for promoting common trade interest then in coming days Asia can become hub of world trade activities. Fortunately, all the three have economic interaction with each other but the need of the hour is to intensify them meaningfully by understanding each other in right perception. They should also take note of unfavourable trend prevalent in developed countries towards exports of developing countries.

Foreign investments in world, both FDI inflows and outflows, are increasing. Particularly FDI outflows of developing countries are going up and the share of ASEAN-5 and China in it is increasing. China with its better network through settled ethnic Chinese in ASEAN-5 sits comfortable in attracting sizeable amount of FDI from the region; while India is much laggard in inflows and outflows. To attract higher doses of FDI from ASEAN-5 and world at large, India needs to turn its economy highly competitive like China by achieving sustainable higher growth in coming years.

Table 2.1
GDP Growth : World, ASEAN and India, 1985-1999 (Percentage change over previous year)

	1985-1990	*1990-1995*	*1996*	*1997*	*1998*	*1999*
World	3.2	1.9	3.3	3.3	2.0	1.9
Industrialized countries	3.2	1.7	2.9	2.9	2.2	1.9
Developing countries	3.1	4.9	5.8	5.4	1.8	2.1
of which Asia	4.4	6.4	7.1	5.8	1.6	3.3
Newly industrializing economies	N.A.	6.9	6.3	6.0	–1.8	3.1
Singapore	N.A.	8.5	6.9	7.8	1.5	0.7
Asean-4	N.A.	7.0	6.9	3.7	– 9.0	– 0.7
India	N.A.	4.5	7.8	5.0	5.8	5.0
China	N.A.	12.4	9.6	8.8	7.8	6.6

Note: (i) Figures for the year 1999 are forecast
(ii) ASEAN – 4 includes Indonesia, Malaysia, Philippines and Thailand
(iii) Newly Industrializing economies include Hong Kong, China, South Korea, Taiwan and Singapore.

Source: UNCTAD 'Trade and Development Report', relevant issues UN, New York.

Table 2.2

Exports and Imports by Major Regional Economic Groupings, 1985-1998
(Percentage change in volume over previous year)

	1985-90	*1990-95*	*1996*	*1997*	*1998*	*1985-90*	*1990-95*	*1996*	*1997*	*1998*
	Exports					**Imports**				
World	6.0	6.0	5.5	10.5	3.5	6.2	6.5	6.0	9.5	4.0
Developed market economy countries	5.3	5.3	5.2	10.2	3.4	6.8	5.6	5.4	8.5	7.4
Developing countries of which	8.4	9.0	6.9	12.3	3.4	6.7	10.1	6.6	10.8	– 4.5
Asia of which	NA	12.6	6.2	12.4	1.4	NA	13.7	5.8	7.0	– 10.1
ASEAN-4	NA	14.8	5.9	13.2	0.8	NA	14.9	4.2	4.7	– 21.9
Newly industrializing economies	NA	12.5	9.1	11.5	3.3	NA	13.2	6.4	7.7	– 11.5
China	10.3	17.2	–.8	20.5	3.6	4.5	17.9	6.5	5.1	3.6
India	11.0	13.0	13.0	– 3.0	12.0	10.0	12.0	16.0	–3.0	5.0

Source: UNCTAD 'Trade and Development Report', relevant years UN, New York.

Table 2.3
FDI Inflows in India, ASEAN and China – 1986-98

(Million US $)

	1986-91 (Annual average)	*1992-98 (Annual average)*	*1992*	*1993*	*1994*	*1995*	*1996*	*1997*	*1998*
World	159331	344765	175841	217559	242999	331189	337550	464341	643879
Developing Countries	29090	113287	51108	72528	95588	105511	129813	172533	84880
Asia	16468	67046	29651	51218	60679	67386	80011	95505	84880
ASEAN	7908	20694	15508	15508	18699	22519	26816	27813	21400
India	177	1676	233	574	973	1964	2382	3351	2258
China	3105	34115	11156	27515	33787	35849	40800	44236	45460
% share of ASEAN in World	5.0	6.0	6.9	7.1	7.7	6.8	7.9	6.0	3.3
% share of India in World	0.1	0.5	0.1	0.3	0.4	0.6	0.7	0.7	0.4
% share of China in World	1.9	10	6.3	12.7	13.9	10.8	12.1	10.0	7.1

Source : UNCTAD 'World Investment Report', relevant issues.

Table 2.4
FDI outflows of India, ASEAN and China – 1986-98

(Million US $)

	1986-91 (Annual average)	*1992-98 (Annual average)*	*1992*	*1993*	*1994*	*1995*	*1996*	*1997*	*1998*
World	180510	370804	200800	247425	284915	358573	379872	475125	648920
Developing Countries	11331	47351	20714	39756	42600	52089	58947	65031	52318
Asia	8975	37973	18786	31476	35886	44060	51681	47741	36182
ASEAN	1067	7566	2035	4631	8572	11281	12160	8918	5365
India	03	85	24	Nil	83	117	239	113	19
China	745	2668	4000	4400	2000	2000	2114	2563	1600
% share of ASEAN in World	0.6	2.04	1.0	1.9	3.0	3.1	3.20	1.88	0.83
% share of India in World	0.002	0.02	0.001	Nil	0.03	0.03	0.06	0.02	0.003
% share of China in World	0.41	0.72	2.00	1.8	0.70	0.56	0.56	0.54	0.25

Source : UNCTAD 'World Investment Report', relevant issues.

NOTES & REFERENCES

1. Here all the figures for trade and foreign investment are annual average and we have purposely done so in order to present overall picture of the period instead of relying on year-based figures. This exercise may make the interpretation more lively and topical and reflect clarity in our analysis. We have divided the entire period of our concern here, i.e. 1985 through 1998, in two parts first 1985-91, and second 1992-98. The part one, i.e. 1985-91 represents the pre-reform and 'pre look-east policy' period and part two, i.e. 1992-98 represents post reform and 'post look-east policy' period. This we have done to highlight the effect of 'look-east policy' on India's interaction with ASEAN by comparing the performance of second part with first part.
2. Stiglitz, Joseph, (1999), "Full Recovery Ahead" an interview in *Far Eastern Economic Review* dated November 4, 1999.

3

India–ASEAN: Trade Interaction

The share of ASEAN-5 in India's exports in 1992-98 has gone up to 8 per cent from 4 per cent in 1985-91. In value terms it increased to US$2163 million annually from US$521 million. Similarly ASEAN-5 share in India's total imports has gone upto 8 per cent in 1992-98 from 5 per cent in 1985-91. Value-wise, it increased to US$2562 million annually from US$1006 million. How did India matter in ASEAN-5 total trade with the world? The ASEAN-5 exports to India in 1992-98 in real terms reduced to 1.14 per cent from 1.30 per cent in 1985-91. However, the ASEAN-5 imports from India in 1992-98 (in real terms) has gone up marginally to 0.91 from 0.80 per cent in 1985-91 [see Table : 3.1 and 3.2].

Over the period ASEAN-5 on the basis of its higher exports (than imports) enjoyed favourable trade balance with India. It implies that though India could increase her exports to ASEAN-5 but simultaneously her imports also increased. The 'look-east policy' made positive impact on India's trade with ASEAN-5, both in real and value terms, but the response of the opposite side was relatively lukewarm. The causes of ASEAN-5 behaviour will be analysed here in details in further discussion.

In this chapter we would analyse (i) India's trade with ASEAN countries by pointing out pre-eminence of ASEAN-5 in their interaction; (ii) India's trade with ASEAN-5 on the basis of import and export intensity indices; (iii) India-ASEAN-5 trade in the context of 'third country' comparison; (iv) commodity structure of India-ASEAN-5 trade; (v) future potentials; and (vi) emerging trend between India-ASEAN-5 trade.

Trade between India and 'other five' ASEAN

How is India's trade interaction with 'other five' countries of ASEAN? The 'five' countries are Brunei, Vietnam, Laos, Myanmar and Cambodia. In 1985-91 India's annual exports to these five countries is US$13 million and the same in 1992-98 increased to US$59 million. India's imports from these countries during the same period is US$99 million and US$134 million, respectively. If these trade figures are compared with the corresponding figures of ASEAN-5 discussed earlier here, then we find these countries are absolutely minuscule in India's trade. Secondly, the thrust of India's 'look-east' policy lies in ASEAN-5 for obvious reasons discussed here in earlier chapters.

Trade between India and ASEAN-5

India's balance of trade over the period, i.e. 1985-91 and 1992-98 with ASEAN-5 continued to remain adverse but the gap between export and import has narrowed down in the latter period, reducing the deficit on trade account: It came down to negative US$399 million in 1992-98 from US$485 million in 1985-91. The deficit has decreased not basically because India's imports slowed down but exports during 1992-98 increased much rapidly. The rise in exports can be attributed to massive devaluation of the Indian rupee effected by the government in, August 1991 to give fillip to exports. Between 1985-91 and 1992-98 Indian exports to and imports from ASEAN-5 increased by 4.2 and 2.6 times, respectively.

The overall trend of two-way trade between India and ASEAN-5 discussed above could by analysed further by considering trade performance of India and individual ASEAN-5 countries.[1] In 1992-98, among ASEAN-5 countries, Singapore is the most important export destination (or market) for the Indian products: the single market absorbing about 34 per cent of Indian exports to ASEAN-5. The corresponding figures for Thailand and Indonesia is 19 per cent each; for Malaysia it is 18 per cent. Even in 1985-91 Singapore was the most important market for Indian exports. Only surprise change is Indonesia which was not so prominent in 1985-91 turned to be one of the important markets for Indian exports. Philippines too gained reasonable significance in 1992-98 for Indian exports which was not so in 1985-91. Thus under 'look east' policy India could increase export penetration in all ASEAN-5 markets.

During 1985-98 the ASEAN-5 export performance in Indian market was much better than vice-versa; hence the substantial trade deficit incurred by India vis-à-vis ASEAN-5. Singapore performed best: increasing its annual exports to India from US$756 million in 1985-91 to US$1699 million in 1992-98. Singapore's share in total export of ASEAN-5 to India in 1992-98 is more than 50 per cent. Thus during 1985-98 Singapore emerged as the most important trading partner of India (followed by Malaysia). Singapore enjoys an annual trade surplus of US$850 million with India.[2] Malaysia too enjoys a trade surplus with India. However, Indonesia, Philippines and Thailand carry a trade deficit with India which can be taken as a positive signal for increasing Indian exports to these three markets. More importantly, the trade pattern of ASEAN-5 with India during 1985-91 and 1992-98 remained the same implying that Singapore and Malaysia will continue to be biggest trade partners in future. It implies that India needs to adopt export strategy on country basis by taking into consideration the prevailing trend of trade pattern with individual country.

Surprisingly since 1997-98 Indonesia has become prominent import sourcing country for India and on the basis of higher exports (than imports) it enjoys trade surplus with

India for the past three years. The trade between two countries has crossed US$ 1 billion mark. Indonesia could increase exports because of depreciation of her currency since July 1997 in the aftermath of financial crisis (See Table: 3.3). India's bilateral trade with Singapore and Malaysia has crossed US$ 2 billion mark in 1999-2000; however its trade with Philippines and Thailand is still below US$ 1 billion.

The above discussion leads to the following questions: (1) Is ASEAN-5 market share in Indian exports and imports growing relatively if seen vis-a-vis other countries? An analysis of trade intensity indices later will answer this question. (2) What caused the accumulation of India's trade deficit vis-avis ASEAN-5 over the period? These and other related questions will be addressed in the discussion on the basis of details of the commodity structure of trade later.

Trade Intensity of India with ASEAN-5

The bilateral trade relations between India and ASEAN-5 countries can be drawn out more sharply with "third country" comparisons;[3] and the changes over time of trade relations between them (i.e. India and ASEAN-5) can be indicated by the use of trade intensity indices.

The intensity of India's export trade with another region/country (ASEAN-5 /Singapore) is measured by the ratio of ASEAN's-5 share in India's exports to ASEAN's-5 share in total world imports less India's imports. Likewise, the intensity of India's import trade with another region (ASEAN-5) is measured by the ratio of ASEAN-5 share in India's imports to ASEAN-5 share in total world exports less India's exports. Therefore, an export intensity of more (or less) than 1.0 indicates that India is exporting more (or less) to a particular region/country than might be expected from the country's share in the world trade total. Similarly, the intensity of India's import trade indicates the extent to which India takes more (or less) imports from a particular region than might be expected from that region's share in world trade. The variation in the value of trade intensity indices may be accounted for by factors including economic complementarity, political and historical ties, investment and aid links, and the competitiveness of country's exports.[4]

The Table : 3.4 shows that India's exports to ASEAN-5 is relatively of high intensity. Over the period 1985-91 and 1992-98, the intensity of India's exports to ASEAN-5 registered a notable rise from the value of 0.98 to 1.26. ASEAN-5 became more important as a market to Indian merchandise compared to other regions (or "third countries"), except USA. It is also noticeable that India's exports to ASEAN-5 in absolute terms has also increased. India's export intensity with "third countries" comparison increased in USA and China but substantially reduced in Japan but still it is close to unity implying that the setback is temporary owing to recessionary situation in Japanese market.

India's export intensity index with USA remained above unity during the entire period underlining the importance of US market for Indian products. In the case of Chinese although intensity index is much less than unity in 1992-98 (i.e. 0.462) yet it has much improved over the previous period of 1985-91 (i.e. 0.097) pointing towards emergence of new trading partner of India in Asia. In terms of individual countries as market for Indian exports, all the countries of ASEAN-5 became significant and with equal measure, especially Indonesia and Philippines surged much ahead in 1990s. The fact that value of India's export intensity index is more than 1.0 in all these five markets in 1992-98 can be seen as a positive signal for enhancing India's future exports.

The Table: 3.5 shows the import performance of Indian-ASEAN-5 trade. Between 1985-91 and 1992-98, India's imports from ASEAN-5 has remained more or less same. In perfect terms the import intensity index has marginally slide down from value 1.36 to 1.34. This also conversely reveals that for ASEAN-5 exports Indian market is equally important. In terms of individual countries, Indian import intensity index has much improved with Indonesia during 1992-98, but descended substantially in the case of Malaysia; and with Philippines and Thailand the index remained more or less the same and below unity. In the case of Singapore the index has reasonably gone up and by staying above unity during 1985-98 indicates the consistent importance of the country as an import sourcing point to India. Most significantly during 1992-98 Indonesia became India's close trading partner like Singapore and Malaysia, in both import as well as export business. This change can be attributed to Indonesian trade policy since 1985 which propagated opening of trade regime.[5]

To see ASEAN-5 significance to India as an import-sourcing market we would adopt "third country" approach. India's import intensity index in 1992-98 reduced in the case of USA and Japan (below unity) and with China it increased reasonably although continued to stay below unity. The decline in indices in developed markets of USA and Japan is an indicative of India moving towards developing countries even to fulfil her import demand and in the process finding new supplier country like China.

ASEAN-5 Trade with USA, Japan and China

Consistent with continuing discussion it would be imperative to find out how ASEAN-5 look at India as a trade partner vis-à-vis 'third countries' comparison. The Table 3.6 displays that in 1985-91 the collective export intensity index of ASEAN-5 in USA, Japan and China is above unity identifying over representation of the 'trio' in ASEAN-5 exports. In 1992-98 the index continued to stay above unity in USA and Japan but decelerated below unity in China. Although Japan fares best during the entire period but the value of index has much declined in 1992-98 pointing out diversion of ASEAN-5 exports to other markets.

The import intensity index of ASEAN-5 vis-à-vis above mentioned 'trio' countries manifests that in 1985-91 the value of index is above unity in all the three markets with Japan topping as an import sourcing country. The index in 1992-98 deteriorated in USA below unity (i.e. 0.91) revealing marginal loss of significance as import supplier to ASEAN-5. In the case of China too the index value in 1990s went down but stayed above unity (i.e. 1.07) signalling reasonable importance as import sourcing country. Japan's significance as principal import sourcing country to all the ASEAN-5 nations continued during 1985-98 [see Table: 3.7]. India's exports to ASEAN-5 in future will mostly depend upon how the 'trio' succeed in penetrating their exports in ASEAN-5 market. Based on index the prevailing trend shows that the 'trio' hold considerable sway as an exporter to ASEAN-5 and Indian export will continue to face competition from the 'trio'. India's export intensity index in ASEAN-5 in 1992-98 has indeed improved nevertheless her exports in (absolute) value terms falls much short of the 'trio'.[6]

Commodity Structure of India – ASEAN-5 Trade

An analysis of the commodity structure of imports and exports by major groups can provide further insights into India's trade relations with ASEAN-5.

The Table 3.8 reveals that rapid industrialization of India during 1980s and 1990s enabled the economy in mounting manufactured exports to ASEAN-5. Between 1988-89 and 1998-99 the share of manufactured exports accelerated to almost all the ASEAN-5 countries with the exception of Indonesia and Philippines where India's manufactures are slightly lower than primary exports. Otherwise in the case of Thailand percentage of manufactured exports in India's total exports (to that country) is 75; in the case of Singapore it is 71; and in the case of Malaysia it is 60. The manufactured export items are mainly machinery and instruments, transport equipment, electronic goods, manufacturers of metals, drugs and pharmaceuticals. In addition to these items, gems and jewellery are also prominent Indian export to Singapore and Thailand [see Table : 3.9]. It is also noteworthy that with the rapid advancement of technology and engineering science, the items of information technology (IT Products) in Indian exports are rising up.

Among India's prominent primary export items to ASEAN-5 include oil meals, rice, meat preparations, fruits and vegetables, marine products, castor oil. Looking at these items, over the years composition of primary export items has not undergone much change and factor of "value addition" (concerned with these products) continues to get neglected.

The Table : 3.10 gives the classified picture of India's imports from ASEAN-5 which depicts that with the beginning of the opening up of domestic import regime the demand for manufactured items gone up and correspondingly that of primary products gone down. The proportion of manufactured items in India's total imports from Singapore and Philippines is 90 per cent each; in the case of Thailand it is 76 per cent; and in case of Indonesia and Malaysia it is 55 and 48 per cent respectively. The principal items of manufactured imports are electronic goods, professional instruments, artificial resins, organic chemicals, electrical machinery, textile yarn and fabrics, synthetic and regenerated fabrics. The list of primary products include edible oils, vegetable oils, non-ferrous metals, wood and wood products, natural rubber and pulp and waste paper [see Table 3.11].

Trade Potentials

The change in the composition of India's exports to and imports from ASEAN-5 indicates that in future the trade between them will be driven by manufactured items. Nevertheless the trade in primary items can not be undermined, especially in case of ASEAN-5 imports from India. India can boost up export of value added agricultural products to ASEAN-5 because with the adoption of advanced technology in bio- informatics Indian manufacturers in this line possess competitive advantage over her competitors. Given the fact that large number of consumers in ASEAN-5 countries are gradually moving into higher middle income group their consumption pattern is also undergoing drastic change and demand for quality agricultural products is rapidly burgeoning. For these consumers the Indian products could be the right choice because of numerous varieties the country produces in large product segments. Already there is awareness about India's capability in manufacturing of quality food products in ASEAN-5 and what is lacking at present is traders sustained campaign of these products in competitive environment. If Indian exporters could do it then obviously their products may find large market in ASEAN-5. In the following lines potential of India and ASEAN-5 trade is given on "one to one basis":

Indonesia

As pointed out here Indonesia has emerged the third largest trading partner of India in ASEAN region in 1990s. The other two largest partners are Singapore and Malaysia. Since 1997-98 Indonesian exports in Indian market are rapidly rising owing to the undervaluation of Indonesian currency in the backdrop of July 1997 financial crisis. And secondly, because of more liberalized trade regime in India since 1991. The trade potential between India and Indonesia lies in resource based products such as agricultural and natural items because both the countries are endowed with rich and varied natural resources.

There is growing awareness in Indonesia about India's competitiveness in agricultural products such as cereals and grains. However, most of the Indonesian agricultural imports are sourced from Australia. Price-wise Australian products are expensive than Indian. There is possibility that Indonesia may switch over to India to import these products as price-wise Indian products are competitive. Similarly Indian sugar could be another item as Indonesian sugar production falls short of its domestic demand and every year large quantity of sugar get imported. Indian sugar exporters can fill this gap. Next item could be Indian marine products. Indonesian demand for quality marine products is increasing and India is one of the exporters to Indonesia. Further meat and meat preparation could be another item. Although Indonesia imports large quantity of these items from other countries but do not source it from India. Its neighbouring countries namely Malaysia and Philippines source this item from India in large quantity. The exporters of this item can explore possibility of selling it in Indonesian market. Indian exporters by adopting internationally approved hygenic standards can enhance export of these products.

In case of Indian industrial and engineering products Indonesia appreciates them being suitable to the Indonesian requirements. Especially manufacturing of machinery for small and medium-sized enterprises (SMEs). For instance, machinery used in the bakery industry. Being a producer of variety of bakery products Indonesia needs modern bakery machinery and obviously Indian manufacturers can supply such machineries to Indonesia. Similarly other machinery and equipments which are required in the SME sector can be supplied by India.

Like other countries Indonesia appreciates India's leap-forward in manufacturing of IT products. Currently the use of IT products in Indonesia is much higher than India. However, India's export of electronic goods to Indonesia is lowest if compared with other ASEAN-5 countries. It was about US $ 3.5 million per annum in 1990s. while in case of Malaysia and Singapore it was US $ 32 million and US $ 86 million per annum respectively. There is need that Indian exporters of these products to sort out proper strategy to tap the growing Indonesian market for electronic goods.

Malaysia

Between 1990 and 1997 Malaysia remained India's second largest trading partner in ASEAN region. However during 1998-99 & 1999-2000 bilateral trade with Malaysia surpassed India's trade with Singapore. The component of Indian import is much higher than her export to Malaysia.

Therefore the trade balance continues to be unfavourable to India. In fact, the trade deficit is rapidly expanding with the depreciation of Malaysian currency (i.e. ringgit) since 1998. Going by the prevailing trend the Malaysian exporters are in advantageous position to reap the benefit of price competitiveness (because of undervaluation of ringgit) and may enhance their exports to India.

Given the rapid surge in Indo-Malaysian trade between 1995-2000, there is immense scope for expanding it further on larger scale. For instance their bilateral trade during 1999-2000 reached to US $ 2.5 billion from US $ 1.3 billion in 1995-96. During the same period India's annual average exports to and imports from Malaysia accounted for 1.27 and 3.22 percent respectively of her (i.e. India's) total exports and imports.

Currently Malaysia's global imports comprises mainly of intermediate goods (about 75 percent) of total imports, capital goods (about 15 percent) and consumption good (about 6 percent). India do have competitive advantage in manufacturing and producing intermediate as well as consumption items, especially electrical and electronic products, cereals, vegetables, oil seeds and fruits, processed food products. Indian exporters by applying proper marketing strategy can obviously enhance exports of these products to Malaysia.

Besides, Indian IT products may find good demand in Malaysian growing market. Currently in Malaysia, there is wide use of IT products in almost all manufacturing and service activities and the country recognises India's achievement in IT sector. Indian manufacturers in IT sector are in advantageous position in increasing export of their products in Malaysia.

Printing and allied industry is a new area in knowledge-based industry which is rapidly surging ahead in India's export business. The export of print material in India is being done on large scale by printers like Thompson Press, Tata

Press. Currently the export of printing machines, pre-press equipment and publish items are being made to USA, CIS, African and South Asian countries. Malaysia these days is investing considerable revenue in higher education and experiencing boom in technical and professional education. This boom in higher education is simultaneously increasing demand for print materials and machinery. Indian businessmen in this activity can tap growing Malaysian market.

Another Indian item which could fetch good demand in Malaysia is spices and spices related food products. With the rise in middle income and higher middle income population the demand for quality and varied spices item is ever growing in Malaysia and already some of the Indian brands are popular there. Indian manufacturers in spices products can obviously enhance their market share on the basis of price and quality competitiveness. Besides, there is increasing demand for spices related machinery like pepper thresher and Indian manufacturers can take advantage of this new rising demand.

Another Indian export-item which could tap large Malaysian demand is meat and meat preparations. Until recently Malaysian market used to get flooded by European meat and meat preparations but the outbreak of mad cow and foot and mouth diseases (FMD) in European livestock Malaysian consumers are looking for new suppliers. Indian suppliers especially in frozen boneless buffalo meat can take advantage and increase the quantity of their exports to Malaysia.

For Indian importers Malaysian items such as palm oil, petroleum crude and products, wood and wood products, electronic goods could be advantageous. Till recently India continued to be the largest importer of Malaysian palm oil. However, the hike in tariff duties since March 2001 has drastically reduced the import of palm oil. Malaysia is pressing for reduction in import duty on palm oil. To find out the way, Indian govt. has entered into counter-trade mechanism with the Malaysian govt. and now palm oil will be imported in exchange of services rendered by the Indian Railway construction company to build railway lines in Malaysia.

Philippines

Throughout 1980s and 1990s India enjoyed favourable trade balance with Philippines. The annual average two way trade between them during 1990s was in the range of US $ 150 to 300 million. Philippines is India's weakest trade partner among ASEAN-5 group. The Filipino exports in the past three years have picked up in Indian market because of undervaluation of its currency, otherwise Filipino exports remained static in Indian market for long period.

Among principal Indian export items to Philippines are meat and meat preparations, manufactures of metals, drugs, pharmaceuticals & fine chemicals, cotton yarn fabrics, madeups and oil meals. India's future export potential lies in items pertaining to drugs and pharmaceutical industry because Philippines recongnises India's achievement in manufacturing of these items and had shown keen interest in establishing joint ventures with Indian counterparts. Similarly Philippines imports considerable quantity of meat and meat preparation from European countries. Given the fact that FMD disease is spreading widely among European livestock in recent period the Indian exporters in this line can take advantage of this situation and proliferate their sale to Philippines. Further Indian exporters in the agricultural and food products such as groundnuts, spices, marine products, poultry and dairy products, oil meals, processed fruits and juices can take advantage of Philippines growing market in these product segment.

Singapore

During 1990s Singapore continued to be India's strongest trade partner within the ASEAN region with average bilateral trade crossing over US $ 2 billion per annum. However, the trade balance always remained unfavourable to India. In their two way trade Indian exports enjoy considerable complementarity with Singapore imports implying that the trade between them is mutually beneficial and therefore in future it could further expand

Wide variety of items continue to dominate India's exports to Singapore. The gems & jewellery and electronic product occupies prominence in India's exports to Singapore. Even the food products such as spices, cashew, non-basmati rice, marine items are also gaining prominence. In recent years printed matter is also rapidly becoming important export item. The increase in food products export is important in the sense that Singapore market occupies special significance in the whole region of Southeast and East Asia and India can use Singapore as a base for marketing these products in other adjacent countries.

Other potential items are handicrafts, glass & glassware, natural silk, RMG of silk. Singapore being an attractive tourist resort a large number of tourist from all over the world visit the country and tourists mostly make purchase of these items. Already some of the Indian brands are popular there. By applying right marketing strategy Indian exporters can certainly multiply sale of these items in coming future.

Under potential imports from Singapore the main items could be electronic goods, mostly IT products, petroleum crude & refined products, scientific and optical instruments, artificial resins and plastic materials.

Thailand

The annual average Indo-Thai bilateral trade during 1990s was in the range of US $ 600 to 800 million. This trade was heavily in favour of India although in the past three years Thailand got the benefit of depreciation of its currency when its exports to India increased but trade balance continued to remain in India's favour. During the entire decade of 1990 a single item which dominated the Indian exports to Thailand was gems & jewellery; its export value being one third of total exports to Thailand. Round the year large number of tourists visit Thailand which fetch good demand for Indian gems & jewellery. In recent years the Thai demand for Indian electronic goods is increasing however its export is comparatively much less than what it is to Malaysia and Singapore.

For Indian exporters, the potential items could be which belong to the category of intermediate of heavy and chemical industry such as nitrogen function compound and synthetic dyes and products falling under capital goods category. The demand for items under these two categories is ever rising in Thailand and Indian manufacturers can reap the advantage of enlarging demand for these products. Currently Indian exports do not commensurate to the large Thai demand and therefore efforts are needed to promote these goods in Thai market.

Emerging Trend

Based on the analyses of import and export intensity indices, the Indian-ASEAN-5 trade for 1985 to 1998 period, has performed satisfactory in comparison to 'third countries', for instance Japan. India's export intensity index with ASEAN-5 in 1992-98 vis-à-vis USA is almost at par and better against Japan. India's import intensity index with ASEAN-5 in 1992-98 is greater than USA and Japan implying relatively high importance of ASEAN-5 in India's import trade. Nevertheless, in absolute value terms India's bilateral trade with both USA and Japan individually, is much greater than collective ASEAN-5 countries.

Between 1988-89 to 1998-99 the commodity structure of India-ASEAN-5 bilateral trade has undergone marked changes. This is especially true in the case of India switching from exporting mainly primary commodities to manufactured products, reflecting the rapid development of the manufacturing sector in the economy. Equally important is the changed composition of India's imports from ASEAN-5 signalling reduction of import tariffs on manufactured items and opening the domestic market for consumer items and asking local to compete with foreign producers.

While Indo-ASEAN-5 trade has been increasing rapidly in recent years, the balance of trade between them is moving overwhelmingly in favour of ASEAN-5. The undervaluation of ASEAN-5 currencies helped them to enhance their exports in world as well as in India. The spurt in their exports may be temporary phenomenon however in the longer run they may stabilise it on the basis of sound network they have established in India. The removal of quantitative restrictions (QRs) from all imports since April 1, 2001 and lowering of import tariff in recent years may further boost up ASEAN-5 exports to India. On the contrary Indian exports may face stiff competition in ASEAN-5 market even though during "look-east policy" the country could able to increase penetration in ASEAN-5. It is mainly because India's price-competitiveness (on the basis of devaluation of its currency) is nullified by relatively steep fall in ASEAN-5 currency value vis-à-vis US dollar. This unusual situation calls for right strategy to be adopted by the Indian exporters while marketing their products in ASEAN-5 region. Not only that but Indian exporters would face competition from ASEAN-5 in their global export business owing to lower prices of ASEAN-5 exports.

What is the way out? The first and foremost is to enhance the quality of export products so that Indian products could get identified with superior quality and ASEAN-5 consumers reveal their preferences to Indian brands. This is especially essential in agricultural and food products[7]. The Chinese products in this segment pose serious competition to the Indian brands because Chinese businessmen have established marketing–chain network through Chinese ethnic settled population in ASEAN-5 which facilitates Chinese trade in the region. In case of manufactured items US and Japan are significant exporters and through their large investment in ASEAN-5 they have established strong network in the region and therefore they have competitive advantage over their Indian counterparts in selling their products. Indian exporters need to explore possibility of establishing manufacturing units in the region to successfully compete with US and Japan in enhancing exports.

End Note:

The degree of bilateral orientation of India's trade with ASEAN-5 countries can be indicated well by the following trade indices. The import intensity of trade of India with individual country of ASEAN-5 is measured by the formula below:

$$mij = \frac{Mij}{Mi} \Big/ \frac{Xj}{Xw - Xi}$$

where Mij is imports of country i from trading partner j,
Mi is total import of country i
X j is total export of country j
Xw is total world exports
Xi is total exports of country i

The import intensity index is derived from the proportion of country is imports sourced from country j, divided by the ratio of country j's exports over total world exports net of country is share. Likewise, the export intensity index of India's trade with individual country of ASEAN-5 is computed as:

$$xij = \frac{Xij}{Xi} \Big/ \frac{Mj}{Mw - Mi}$$

where xij is the exports of country i to trading partner j,
Xi is total exports of country i
M j is total imports of country j
Mw is total world imports
Mi is total imports of country i

Table 3.1
India's Imports and Exports and Balance of Trade with ASEAN (annual average), 1985-91 and 1992-1998

(US $ million)

	Indonesia		Philippines		Malaysia		Singapore	
	1985-91	1992-98	1985-91	1992-98	1985-91	1992-98	1985-91	1992-98
India								
Export	52	407	21	231	102	385	236	728
Import	73	386	11	42	475	826	390	1147
Balance of Trade	-21	21	10	189	-373	-441	-154	-419
	Thailand		**ASEAN-5**		**Brunei**		**Vietnam**	
	1985-91	1992-98	1985-91	1992-98	1985-91	1992-98	1985-91	1992-98
Export	110	412	521	2163	0.14	2	12	44
Import	57	161	1006	2562	Nil	Nil	36	27
Balance of Trade	53	251	-485	-399	0.14	2	-24	17
	Laos		**Myanmar**		**Cambodia**		**ASEAN**	
	1985-91	1992-98	1985-91	1992-98	1985-91	1992-98	1985-91	1992-98
Export	NA	NA	1.43	13	0.14	0.71	534	2222
Import	NA	NA	63	98	NA	9.57	1105	2696
Balance of Trade	NA	NA	-61.57	-85	0.14	-8.86	-571	-474

Source : IMF, 'Direction of Trade Stastics Year Book' - relevant issues.

Table 3.2
ASEAN -5 Imports and Exports and Balance of Trade with India (annual average) 1985-91 and 1992-98

(US $ million)

	INDIA			INDIA	
	1985-91	1992-98		1985-91	1992-98
Indonesia			**Singapore**		
Export	57	385	Export	756	1699
Import	84	463	Import	285	819
Balance of Trade	-27	-78	Balance of Trade	471	880
Malaysia			**Thailand**		
Export	424	816	Export	87	211
Import	166	563	Import	308	544
Balance of Trade	258	253	Balance of Trade	-221	-333
Philippines			**ASEAN-5**		
Export	21	70	Export	1345	3181
Import	36	275	Import	879	2664
Balance of Trade	-15	-205	Balance of Trade	466	517

Source : IMF 'Direction of Trade Statistics Year Book', relevant issues.

Table 3.3
India's Imports and Exports and Balance of Trade with ASEAN-5 (1997-98 to 1999-2000)

(US $ million)

	Indonesia			Malaysia			Philippines		
Year	1997-98	98-99	99-2000	97-98	98-99	99-2000	97-98	98-99	99-2000
India									
Export	437.78	185.23	326.83	490.49	321.63	435.52	239.01	118.71	143.76
Import	732.51	828.92	991.97	1180.32	1610.38	2059.34	27.77	37.25	56.67
Balance of trade	-294.73	-643.69	-665.14	-689.83	-1288.75	-1623.82	211.24	81.46	87.09
	Singapore			**Thailand**					
	1997-98	98-99	99-2000	97-98	98-99	99-2000			
Export	780.65	517.33	692.01	344.90	320.92	457.26			
Import	1199.33	1383.85	1508.28	233.60	273.05	321.34			
Balance of Trade	-418.68	-866.52	-816.27	111.3	47.87	135.92			

Source: CMIE 'India: Foreign Trade and Balance of Payments', July 2000, Mumbai.

Note: Indian Fiscal Year

Table 3.4
India — Asean-5 Export Intensity Indices, 1985-91 and 1992-98

	Indonesia	Philippines	Malaysia	Singapore	Thailand	ASEAN-5
INDIA (exporter)						
1985-91	0.68	0.49	1.04	1.13	1.08	0.98
19921-98	1.99	1.34	1.02	1.16	1.23	1.26

India - USA, Japan and China Export Intensity Indices, 1985-91 & 1992-98

	USA	Japan	China
INDIA (exporter)			
1985-91	1.07	1.53	0.097
1992-98	1.29	0.99	0.462

Source : Derived from Annexures 3. A through 3.E of this book.
Note : Author's Own Computation.

Table 3.5
India-ASEAN-5 Export Intensity Indices, 1985-91 and 1992-98

	Indonesia	Philippines	Malaysia	Singapore	Thailand	ASEAN-5
INDIA (importer)						
1985-91	0.49	0.24	3.01	1.44	0.50	1.36
19921-98	1.28	0.32	1.84	1.65	0.48	1.34

India - USA, Japan and China Import Intensity Indices, 1985-91 & 1992-98

	USA	Japan	China
INDIA (exporter)			
1985-91	0.87	1.13	0.25
1992-98	0.71	0.82	0.76

Source : Derived from Annexures 3. A through 3.E of this book.
Note : Author's Own Computation.

Table 3.6
ASEAN-5 - USA, Japan and China Export Intensity Indices, 1985-91 and 1992-98

	USA		JAPAN		CHINA	
	1985-91	*1992-98*	*1985-91*	*1992-98*	*1985-91*	*1992-98*
ASEAN-5 (Exporter)	1.4	1.5	3.13	2.25	1.03	0.78
Indonesia	0.996	1.02	6.304	3.85	1.31	1.20
Philippines	2.23	2.48	2.92	2.28	0.651	0.373
Malaysia	1.02	1.36	2.68	1.77	0.93	0.74
Singapore	1.33	1.28	1.30	1.04	1.11	0.793
Thailand	1.26	1.36	2.46	2.31	1.17	0.77

Source : Derived from Annexures 3. A through 3.E of this book.
Note : Author's Own Computation.

Table 3.7

ASEAN-5 - USA, Japan and China Export Intensity Indices, 1985-91 and 1992-98

	USA		JAPAN		CHINA	
	1985-91	*1992-98*	*1985-91*	*1992-98*	*1985-91*	*1992-98*
ASEAN-5 (Importer)	1.13	0.91	2.93	2.99	1.70	1.07
Indonesia	1.10	0.85	3.19	2.89	1.71	1.32
Philippines	1.79	1.35	2.27	2.76	1.38	0.87
Malaysia	1.42	1.18	2.99	3.11	1.32	0.88
Singapore	0.35	0.27	2.57	2.52	2.31	1.26
Thailand	0.98	0.92	3.61	3.67	1.75	1.03

Source : Derived from Annexures 3. A through 3.E of this book.
Note : Author's Own Computation.

Table 3.8

India's Exports of Primary & Manufacturing items to ASEAN-5 Countries, 1988-89 to 1998-99

(Rupee Crores)

	Total 1988-89 to 1998-99 (average annual)	Per centage in Total	1988-89	89-90	90-91	91-92	92-93	93-94	94-95	95-96	96-97	97-98	1998-99
	(1)	(2)	(3)	(4)	(5)	(6)	(7)	(8)	(9)	(10)	(11)	(12)	13
Indonesia													
Primary	474	56	7	18	068	190	192	381	426	1501	1258	845	326
Manufactures	379	44	39	80	127	173	208	351	428	711	817	773	460
Total	853	100	46	98	195	363	400	732	854	2212	2075	1618	786
Malaysia													
Primary	349	40	64	80	109	211	236	347	356	540	731	627	538
Manufactures	522	60	66	96	159	286	306	425	538	771	1131	1162	799
Total	871	100	130	176	268	497	542	772	894	1311	1862	1789	1337
Philippines													
Primary	159	51	17	10	09	101	63	58	165	287	374	406	253
Manufactures	155	49	19	33	40	057	95	126	147	195	275	470	246
Total	314	100	36	43	49	158	158	184	312	482	649	876	499

Contd....

Table 3.8 (Contd.)

	(1)	(2)	(3)	(4)	(5)	(6)	(7)	(8)	(9)	(10)	(11)	(12)	(13)
Singapore													
Primary	529	29	64	80	118	258	569	840	533	847	1267	734	513
Manufactures	1315	71	261	387	561	697	1132	1520	1863	2202	2154	2012	1675
Total	1844	100	325	667	479	955	1701	2360	2396	3049	3421	2746	2188
Thailand													
Primary	232	25	05	015	083	79	211	369	366	341	440	361	283
Manufactures	707	75	187	302	360	410	521	744	914	1245	1137	894	1062
Total	939	100	192	317	443	489	732	1113	1280	1586	1577	1255	1345
Overall exports of India to World			2,0281	27682	32527	43828	53351	69547	82338	106465	117525	126286	141604

Source : DGCI & S 'Foreign Trade Statistics of India's Principal Commodities and Countries', Calcutta, India, Various relevant issues.

Note : Unit Conversion of Indian Currency Rupee - 10,000,000 (ten million) = one crore or 1000,000,000 (one billion) = 1 hundred crore.

Table 3.9
Top Ten Export Commodities of India to ASEAN-5, 1988-89 To 1998-99

(Rupee Crore)

	1988 -89	*1992 -93*	*1995 -96*	*1998 -99*		*1988 -89*	*1992 -93*	*1995 -96*	*1998 -99*
INDONESIA					MALAYSIA				
(1) Oil meals	02	105	340	217	(1) Meat & preparations	34	93	182	176
(2) Machineray & instruments	–	33	129	55	(2) Cotton yarn, Fabrics	11	43	101	97
(3) Inorganic & Organic Chemicals	–	18	60	45	(3) Fruits & Vegetables	13	25	67	40
(4) Manufactures of Metals	–	11	46	46	(4) Oil meals	04	51	121	137
(5) Dyes/intermediates & coar tar	–	34	60	42	(5) Machinery & instruments	–	56	77	110
(6) Primary & Semi-finished iron & steel	–	–	143	73	(6) Transport equipment	–	32	36	42
(7) Groundnut	–	–	105	29	(7) Electronic Goods	–	–	159	50
(8) Sugar & Malasses	–	10	118	–	(8) Manufactures of Metals	–	54	72	–
(9) Rice (other than Basmati)	–	–	831	–	(9) Drugs & Pharmaceuticals	–	14	–	60
(10) Iron and Steel	–	–	48	–	(10) Marine Products	05	13	52	–
Overall Exports	46	400	2212	786	**Overall exports**	130	542	1311	1337
PHILIPPINES					**SINGAPORE**				
(1) Oil Meals	03	60	132	35	(1) Gems & Jewellary	36	144	324	237
(2) Cotton Yarn, Fabrics	03	09	31	26	(2) Cotton yarn, Fabrics	27	65	111	74

Contd....

Table 3.9 (Contd.)

	1988 -89	1992 -93	1995 -96	1998 -99		1988 -89	1992 -93	1995 -96	1998 -99
PHILIPPINES									
(3) Manufactures of Metals	–	08	30	25	(3) Oil Meals	–	375	409	177
(4) Machinery & instruments	–	22	18	20	(4) Electronic Goods	–	104	458	311
(5) Drugs & Pharmaceuticals	–	07	14	44	(5) Manufactures of Metals	–	98	86	118
(6) Meat & Preparations	–	–	69	113	(6) Machinery and Instruments	–	52	104	121
(7) Rice (other than Basmati)	–	–	48	55	(7) Marine Products	21	51	–	67
(8) Primary & Semi-finished iron & steel	–	–	31	13	(8) Aluminium other than products	–	–	117	74
(9) Inorganic/organic chemicals	–	–	09	18	(9) Rubber Manufactured Products	–	61	78	–
(10) Rubber Manufactured Products	–	07	–	10	(10) Readymade cotton	09	–	68	66
Overall Exports	36	158	482	499	**Overall Exports**	325	1701	3049	2188
THAILAND									
(1) Gems & Jewellary	126	222	766	509					
(2) Oil Meals	04	149	213	125					
(3) Machinery & Instruments	–	33	49	78					
(4) Drugs & Pharmaceuticals	–	25	47	79					

Contd. ...

Table 3.9 (Contd.)

	1988 -89	*1992 -93*	*1995 -96*	*1998 -99*
THAILAND				
(5) Manufactures of Metals	–	18	50	48
(6) Dyes intermediaries & Coal Tar	–	34	45	35
(7) Inorganic/organic Chemicals	–	26	51	49
(8) Marine Products	–	–	55	111
(9) Castor Oil	–	–	31	27
(10) Cotton raw	–	47	–	–
Overall Exports	192	732	1586	1345

Source : Derived from Annexures 3. A through 3.E of this book.
Note : Author's Own Computation.

Table 3.10
India' Imports of Primary & Manufacturing Items from ASEAN-5 (1988-89 to 1998-99)

(Rupees Crore)

	Total 1988-99 to 1998-99 (average annual)	*Per cent-age in Total*	*1988-89*	*89-90*	*90-91*	*91-92*	*92-93*	*93-94*	*94-95*	*95-96*	*96-97*	*97-98*	*1998-99*
	(1)	(2)	(3)	(4)	(5)	(6)	(7)	(8)	(9)	(10)	(11)	(12)	(13)
Indonesia													
Primary	488	45	44	49	093	053	053	126	340	728	772	1113	1997
Manufactures	592	55	47	51	052	108	118	250	663	837	1359	1599	1428
Total	1080	100	91	100	145	161	171	376	1003	1565	2131	2712	3425
Malaysia													
Primary	1157	52	415	193	271	454	411	281	573	1956	2045	2202	3929
Manufactures	1066	48	373	457	728	507	763	495	955	1006	1563	2203	2677
Total	2223	100	788	650	999	961	1174	776	1528	2962	3608	4405	6606
Philippines													
Primary	05	9	0.2	1.0	02	04	02	05	14	12	05	003	007
Manufacturer	49	91	6.8	20.0	08	73	26	14	23	60	54	101	147
Total	54	100	7.0	21	10	77	28	19	37	72	59	104	154

Contd. ...

Table 3. 10 (Contd.)

	(1)	(2)	(3)	(4)	(5)	(6)	(7)	(8)	(9)	(10)	(11)	(12)	(13)
Singapore													
Primary	248	10	47	061	077	130	165	155	436	301	489	491	373
Manufactures	2360	90	573	839	1354	1572	1658	1795	2232	3391	3294	3924	5331
Total	2608	100	620	900	1431	1702	1823	1950	2668	3692	3783	4415	5704
Thailand													
Primary	102	24	034	118	045	26	38	55	301	199	72	121	116
Manufactures	329	76	187	030	071	94	129	123	228	364	626	735	1024
Total	431	100	221	148	116	120	167	178	529	563	698	856	1140
Overall imports of India to World			27693	35412	43171	47797	62923	72806	88705	121647	136844	151554	176099

Source: DGCI & S 'Foreign Trade Statistics of India, Principal Commodities and Countries' Calcutta, India, various relevant issues.

Table 3.11
Top Ten Export Commodities of India to ASEAN-5, 1988-89 To 1998-99 (Rupee Crore)

	1988-89	*1992-93*	*1995-96*	*1998-99*		*1988-89*	*1992-93*	*1995-96*	*1998-99*
INDONESIA					**MALAYSIA**				
(1) Vegetable Oils fixec (edible)	43	–	210	1197	(1) Vegetable Oils fixed (edible)	331	32	1498	3431
(2) Cole, Coke & Briquittes, etc.	01	06	291	297	(2) Non-ferrous metals	21	23	74	101
(3) Organic Chemicals	01	–	172	156	(3) Wood & Wood products	–	333	251	395
(4) Artificial resins	03	–	36	93	(4) Metalifers Ores	–	26	52	51
(5) Pulp and waste paper	–	10	55	86	(5) Machinery except electrical	03	–	25	93
(6) Textile yarn fabrics	–	–	78	102	(6) Chemical material & products	02	07	17	–
(7) Dyeing/Training	–	30	–	68	(7) Electronic machinery	–	13	189	–
(8) Cashewnuts	–	31	60	–	(8) Natural Rubbers	–	13	114	–
(9) Inorganic chemicals	07	23	49	–	(9) Electronic Goods	–	–	–	509
(10) Metalifrs-Ores	–	–	–	177	(10) Transport equipments	–	–	–	227
Overall Exports	91	171	1565	3425	**Overall exports**	788	1174	2962	6606
PHILIPPINES					**SINGAPORE**				
(1) Inorganic chemicals	0.04	19	–	41	(1) Electrical machinary	161	211	109	112
(2) Organic chemicals	01.0	–	07	12	(2) Machinery except electrical	117	191	266	338

Contd....

Table 3.11 (Contd.)

	1988-89	1992-93	1995-96	1998-99		1988-89	1992-93	1995-96	1998-99
PHILIPPINES									
(3) Machinery except electrical	0.20	–	06	05	(3) Organic Chemicals	21	37	303	278
(4) Electrical Machinery	–	02	–	08	(4) Artificial resins	27	41	91	142
(5) Electric goods	–	–	10	35	(5) Non ferrous metals	22	34	89	72
(6) Professional instruments	–	04	05	–	(6) Metalifers Ores and metal scarp	11	80	130	254
(7) Non-ferrous metals	–	–	–	12	(7) Professional instruments	09	33	58	116
(8) Newsprint	–	–	–	07	(8) Electronic Goods	–	–	860	1520
(9) Artificial resins, etc.	–	–	13	–	(9) Transport Equipment	17	–	74	–
(10) Leather	–	–	13	–	(10) Gold & Silver	–	–	–	88
Overall Exports	7.0	28	72	154	**Overall Exports**	620	1831	3692	5704
THAILAND									
(1) Natural Rubber	–	22	90	36					
(2) Machinery except electric	–	17	34	57					
(3) Pearls, precious stones	02	27	29	–					
(4) Inorganic Chemicals	01	12	19	–					
(5) Electrical Machinery	01	06	13	–					

Contd....

Table 3.11 (Contd.)

	1988-89	*1992-93*	*1995-96*	*1998-99*
THAILAND				
(6) Artificial resins, etc.	–	–	60	154
(7) Textile Yarn fabrics	–	–	82	135
(8) Electronic Goods	–	–	59	120
(9) Synthetic & regenerated fibres	–	–	68	46
(10) Pulp and Waste paper	06	–	27	–
Overall Imports	221	167	563	1140

Source : Derived from Annexures 3. A through 3.E of this book.
Note : Author's Own Computation.

Annexure 3.A

India's Imports from and Exports to ASEAN 1985-98

(US $ million)

	1985-91 Total	*1992-98 Total*	*1985*	*86*	*87*	*88*	*89*	*90*	*91*	*1992*	*93*	*94*	*95*	*96*	*97*	*1998*
	(1)	*(2)*	*(3)*	*(4)*	*(5)*	*(6)*	*(7)*	*(8)*	*(9)*	*(10)*	*(11)*	*(12)*	*(13)*	*(14)*	*(15)*	*(16)*
Brunei																
Import	Nil	Nil	Nil	Nil	Nil	Nil	Nil	Nil	Nil	Nil	Nil	Nil	Nil	Nil	NA	NA
Export	1	14	Nil	Nil	Nil	Nil	Nil	Nil	1	1	Nil	1	5	7	NA	NA
Indonesia																
Import	514	2703	38	77	52	54	53	173	67	73	88	283	384	433	703	739
Export	364	2846	11	17	20	25	54	92	145	143	200	253	501	610	596	543
Philippines																
Import	74	292	9	5	6	6	13	4	31	13	7	10	15	196	23	28
Export	147	1615	4	5	11	18	24	21	64	77	48	95	122	741	245	287
Malaysia																
Import	3328	5782	403	395	575	658	360	546	391	534	227	432	770	1228	1218	1373
Export	712	2698	60	64	70	84	105	126	203	222	232	250	355	552	528	559
Singapore																
Import	2732	8026	321	253	310	356	492	689	311	689	593	720	966	1785	1121	2152
Export	1649	5095	103	173	188	223	268	308	386	515	727	738	807	770	892	646

Contd....

Annexure: 3.A (Contd.)

	(1)	(2)	(3)	(4)	(5)	(6)	(7)	(8)	(9)	(10)	(11)	(12)	(13)	(14)	(15)	(16)
Thailand																
Import	397	1130	68	57	38	46	77	62	49	67	54	146	146	264	208	245
Export	773	2885	22	38	59	85	169	201	199	242	318	374	461	570	460	460
Vietnam																
Import	252	186	6	5	8	10	126	59	38	59	44	50	15	18	NA	NA
Export	84	305	13	13	9	17	11	8	13	19	22	43	97	124	NA	NA
Laos																
Import	NA	NA	NA	NA	NA	NA	NA	NA	NA	NA	NA	NA	NA	NA	NA	NA
Export	NA	NA	NA	NA	NA	NA	NA	NA	NA	NA	NA	NA	NA	NA	NA	NA
Myanmar																
Import	441	683	26	29	31	39	175	90	51	104	117	120	160	182	NA	NA
Export	10	90	2	1	1	1	Nil	1	4	4	14	24	21	27	NA	NA
Cambodia																
Import	NA	67	NA	NA	NA	NA	NA	Nil	Nil	3	2	Nil	29	33	NA	NA
Export	1	5	NA	NA	NA	NA	NA	1	Nil	Nil	Nil	1	2	2	NA	NA
ASEAN																
Import	7738	18869	871	821	1020	1169	1296	1623	938	1542	1132	1761	2485	4139	3273	4537
Export	3741	15553	215	311	358	453	631	758	1015	1223	1561	1779	2371	3403	2721	2495

Source : IMF, *'Direction of Trade Statistics Year Book'*, relevant issues.

Annexure 3.B
ASEAN -5 Imports from and Exports to India 1985-98

(US $ million)

	1985-91 Total	*1992-98 Total*	*1985*	*86*	*87*	*88*	*89*	*90*	*91*	*1992*	*93*	*94*	*95*	*96*	*97*	*1998*
Indonesia																
Import	587	3243	15	25	30	46	94	151	226	216	335	315	476	587	703	611
Export	396	2693	43	56	64	67	50	60	56	70	100	283	377	424	692	747
Malaysia																
Import	1162	3943	99	85	99	119	261	215	284	355	398	411	549	740	741	749
Export	2970	5713	432	354	515	539	333	478	319	430	214	527	821	1270	1175	1276
Philippines																
Import	254	1928	6	9	10	29	34	87	79	85	111	147	176	823	270	316
Export	146	493	16	5	5	71	30	2	17	9	226	13	20	179	21	25
Singapore																
Import	1995	5733	221	160	250	265	304	374	421	533	676	790	921	1012	1048	753
Export	5294	11892	485	472	557	737	936	1103	1004	935	955	1261	1877	2072	2285	2507
Thailand																
Import	2154	3808	36	54	94	171	318	544	937	335	522	528	629	640	594	560
Export	606	1475	70	52	45	223	90	63	63	65	74	193	290	242	294	317

Source: IMF 'Direction of Trade Statistics Year Book', relevant issues.

Annexure 3.C
Export of India, ASEAN and Some Prominent Economies, 1984 to 1998

(US $ million)

	1985-91 (Annual average)	*1992-98 (Annual average)*	*1984*	*1985*	*86*	*87*	*88*	*89*
India	13176	28346	9916	8265	9135	10798	12981	15365
Brunei	2134	2239	3183	2934	1798	1901	1707	1921
Indonesia	20964	44238	21881	18597	14809	17170	19376	21936
Philippines	6706	18854	5343	4614	4807	5696	7034	7754
Malaysia	22470	65645	16563	15408	13977	17934	21096	25049
Singapore	38581	101913	24070	22812	22501	28696	39318	44769
Thailand	16503	49076	7414	7123	8864	11564	15910	20175
Vietnam	569	5160	238	342	341	424	532	969
Laos	50	361	11	17	14	23	56	93
Myanmar	302	1051	301	303	288	219	147	215
Cambodia	20	602	46	05	03	10	08	17
USA	311627	628961	217889	213146	217292	252884	319413	363807
Japan	210520	359108	169748	177189	210718	231332	264961	274597
China	47650	132799	24824	27329	31367	39464	47663	52914
World	2662257	4748143	1781000	1812700	1984800	2352600	2690300	2909200

Contd....

Annexure: 3.C (Contd.)

	1990	*1991*	*1992*	*93*	*94*	*95*	*96*	*97*	*1998*
India	17813	17872	18498	20258	24195	30537	34407	33248	37278
Brunei	2212	2466	2496	2362	2106	2084	2329	2344	1953
Indonesia	25681	29178	33967	36823	38289	44004	48059	53440	55082
Philippines	8194	8840	9829	11271	13433	17371	20543	28465	31066
Malaysia	29420	34405	40709	47128	58749	73722	78246	78689	82272
Singapore	52753	59219	63475	74071	96911	118187	125118	125317	110311
Thailand	23072	28811	32472	37158	45733	56432	55789	57560	58387
Vietnam	527	846	1108	1243	1767	3443	4270	11750	12540
Laos	64	82	103	184	438	350	333	560	560
Myanmar	410	530	687	855	914	1183	1274	1168	1276
Cambodia	42	57	165	265	241	350	332	1420	1440
USA	393106	421743	447366	465353	512397	582526	622945	866840	905300
Japan	287664	314845	339864	362583	395201	443005	411242	305000	256860
China	62876	71940	85492	91611	120822	148892	151093	164780	166900
World	3386100	3500100	3751100	3718500	4246800	5069000	5265800	5628300	5557500

Source: IMF 'Direction of Trade Statistics Year Book', relevant issues.

Annexure 3.D
India's Imports from and Exports to ASEAN 1985-98

(US $ million)

	1985-91 (Annual average)	*1992-98 (Annual average)*	*1984*	*1985*	*1986*	*1987*	*1988*	*1989*
India	18584	32220	14361	16329	15051	16841	19130	19239
Brunei	893	3297	622	606	653	641	744	1498
Indonesia	15963	34916	13880	10275	10724	12850	13489	16467
Philippines	9039	29693	6262	5351	5211	6937	8662	11171
Malaysia	20129	64590	14057	12301	10828	12701	16567	22589
Singapore	43595	107613	28667	26237	25513	32626	43869	49694
Thailand	21204	56963	10415	9260	9165	12998	20298	25373
Vietnam	1253	8153	509	610	590	615	794	841
Laos	104	434	36	54	60	80	102	126
Myanmar	433	1988	448	283	304	268	244	194
Cambodia	33	1126	04	27	11	13	24	40
USA	450311	705411	341170	361620	387075	424068	459775	493324
Japan	182586	333310	136142	130516	127660	150907	187483	209635
China	51602	165134	25953	42480	43247	43222	55352	59140
World	2755157	4873271	1844000	1890400	2063800	2420300	2771900	3001400

Contd....

Annexure: 3.D (Contd.)

	1990	*1991*	*1992*	*1993*	*1994*	*1995*	*1996*	*1997*	*1998*
India	23990	19509	23227	21482	25981	34456	40090	39080	41224
Brunei	1000	1111	2430	2600	3124	3490	4689	3923	2821
Indonesia	22008	25928	27280	28328	30387	40236	42945	42851	32383
Philippines	12993	12945	14562	17638	22534	28282	31756	48509	44567
Malaysia	29170	36749	39927	45616	59555	77614	77797	80082	71540
Singapore	60954	66271	71846	85041	102642	124394	131506	131839	106023
Thailand	33408	37925	40686	46065	54394	70382	73484	62804	50923
Vietnam	2841	2483	3027	3924	5826	11695	13668	9310	9620
Laos	149	154	258	352	642	656	639	260	220
Myanmar	668	1068	1057	1247	1590	2319	2482	2696	2526
Cambodia	56	62	751	981	1152	1562	1666	750	1020
USA	517018	509299	552599	600007	689310	770947	817785	765560	741670
Japan	235289	236612	232809	241604	274123	335937	349508	464560	434630
China	53915	63855	81843	103552	115629	132063	138822	288840	295190
World	3510900	3627400	3882000	3777500	4310400	5140700	5401000	5790900	5810400

Source: IMF 'Direction of Trade Statistics Year Book', relevant issues.

Annexure 3.E
Trade of ASEAN-5 and India with USA, Japan and China, 1985-98

(US $ Million)

	USA							
	1985-91 (Annual average)	*1992-98 (Annual average)*	*1985*	*86*	*87*	*88*	*89*	*90*
Indonesia								
Import	2069	3947	1721	1482	1415	1734	2216	2520
Export	3397	6578	4040	2902	3349	3138	3475	3365
Philippines								
Import	1879	5338	1344	1293	1539	1823	2132	2538
Export	2447	6797	1658	1709	2060	2512	2935	3104
Malaysia								
Import	3370	10253	1881	2034	2376	2925	3803	4944
Export	3769	13079	1970	2297	2972	3663	4684	4986
Singapore								
Import	6892	17522	3988	3819	4786	6824	8522	9801
Export	8540	19288	4830	5257	7000	9370	10432	11215
Thailand								
Import	2453	6999	1052	1312	1620	2753	2842	3600
Export	3434	9809	1402	1606	2163	3200	4358	5240
India								
Import	1895	3034	1770	1430	1503	1723	2310	2635
Export	2310	5338	1563	1778	2114	2507	2590	2694

Contd....

Annexure: 3.E (Contd.)

	USA							
	1991	*1992*	*93*	*94*	*95*	*96*	*97*	*1998*
Indonesia								
Import	3397	3822	3255	3424	4579	4361	5671	2520
Export	3509	4419	5230	6179	6476	7948	7212	8583
Philippines								
Import	2610	2626	3532	4162	5225	6243	8170	7411
Export	3151	3843	4342	5178	6217	6966	9816	11214
Malaysia								
Import	5626	6331	7725	9900	12657	12143	13165	9849
Export	5808	7594	9580	12448	15313	14245	14625	17745
Singapore								
Import	10501	11882	13955	15630	18725	21561	22385	18517
Export	11674	13396	15074	18093	21576	23062	23122	20692
Thailand								
Import	3989	4776	5379	6450	8507	9240	8670	5971
Export	6068	7303	8005	9526	10078	10026	11154	12571
India								
Import	1891	2258	2171	2432	3344	3634	3432	3968
Export	2922	3533	3885	4661	5305	5858	6440	7681

Contd....

Annexure: 3.E (Contd.)

	JAPAN							
	1985-91 (Annual average)	*1992-98 (Annual average)*	*1985*	*86*	*87*	*88*	*89*	*90*
Indonesia								
Import	4058	7701	2644	3128	3596	3427	3832	5455
Export	8809	11721	8594	6644	7393	8088	9252	10923
Philippines								
Import	1625	6230	750	887	1149	1503	2174	2397
Export	1300	2958	875	852	980	1416	1581	1622
Malaysia								
Import	4814	15418	2833	2221	2750	3816	5438	7055
Export	4015	8040	3784	3257	3504	3577	4016	4506
Singapore								
Import	8980	20968	4486	5078	6675	9632	10612	12263
Export	3378	7411	2148	1931	2598	3394	3828	4616
Thailand								
Import	6094	15959	2450	2421	3376	5493	7736	10144
Export	2716	7838	951	1260	1732	2545	3422	3970
India								
Import	1663	2008	1364	1931	1742	1943	1494	1801
Export	1343	1933	921	1017	1198	1418	1535	1656

Contd....

Annexure: 3.E (Contd.)

	JAPAN							
	1991	*1992*	*93*	*94*	*95*	*96*	*97*	*1998*
Indonesia								
Import	6327	6014	6248	8250	9863	9965	8484	5085
Export	10767	10761	11172	11465	12348	13839	12543	9920
Philippines								
Import	2517	3087	4022	5447	6303	6916	9564	8271
Export	1771	1745	1811	2020	2740	3668	4558	4161
Malaysia								
Import	9582	10379	12533	15907	21179	19236	17340	11350
Export	5458	5401	6113	7010	9199	10484	9882	8193
Singapore								
Import	14115	15202	18663	22511	26308	23869	23282	16939
Export	5133	4825	5526	6766	9219	10254	8850	6436
Thailand								
Import	11038	11905	13963	16442	21625	20449	16165	11164
Export	5135	5686	6300	7728	9477	9373	8733	7571
India								
Import	1364	1504	1376	1840	2234	2637	1829	2638
Export	1654	1523	1657	1924	2130	2505	1863	1926

Contd....

Annexure: 3.E (Contd.)

	CHINA							
	1985-91 (Annual average)	*1992-98 (Annual average)*	*1985*	*86*	*87*	*88*	*89*	*90*
Indonesia								
Import	490	1299	249	337	408	410	537	653
Export	517	1815	84	139	343	492	534	834
Philippines								
Import	223	722	291	121	217	266	242	182
Export	82	240	81	101	88	67	50	62
Malaysia								
Import	480	1605	251	282	374	482	609	561
Export	394	1675	161	163	279	415	481	619
Singapore								
Import	1832	3875	2268	1430	1412	1691	1698	2095
Export	813	2805	333	571	737	1193	1199	799
Thailand								
Import	667	1659	223	263	504	679	744	1107
Export	365	1289	271	276	388	475	541	269
India								
Import	85	688	104	143	110	128	55	31
Export	24	447	21	08	08	23	43	18

Contd....

Annexure: 3.E (Contd.)

	CHINA							
	1991	*1992*	*93*	*94*	*95*	*96*	*97*	*1998*
Indonesia								
Import	835	752	936	1215	1586	1571	1638	1396
Export	1191	1396	1249	1419	1761	2081	2329	2471
Philippines								
Import	243	184	182	320	660	653	1468	1584
Export	128	114	167	164	209	328	298	401
Malaysia								
Import	802	975	1096	1363	1709	1875	2270	1949
Export	639	772	1204	1933	1889	1882	1868	2180
Singapore								
Import	2227	2253	2404	2885	4042	4441	5668	5429
Export	858	1113	1905	2098	2759	3394	4053	4314
Thailand								
Import	1149	1219	905	1388	2096	1953	2260	1791
Export	335	386	430	930	1642	1868	1744	2025
India								
Import	21	94	259	622	811	758	1062	1209
Export	48	94	286	215	283	655	645	953

Source: As per Annexure 3.A here.

NOTES & REFERENCES

1. For classified data concerning India's trade with individual ASEAN countries in 1985-98, see Annexure: 3.A.
2. For classified data regarding ASEAN-5 trade with India in 1985-98, see Annexure: 3.B.
3. Under "third country" concept here we are taking USA, Japan and China as all these three countries have substantial trade linkages with both India and ASEAN-5.
4. For trade intensity formula and other related details, see note in the end of this chapter.
5. Rachain Chintayarangsan, et al. (1992), 'ASEAN Economies, Macro-Economic Perspective' in *ASEAN Economic Bulletin*, Singapore, vol. 8, No. 3, pp. 353-375.
6. For calculating these various trade intensity indices the classified data is given in Annexures: 3. C, 3. D and 3. E.
7. Ambatkar, Sanjay (2002) "Trade-led Strategy of India in ASEAN" in *Margin*, issue of January to March.

4

India-ASEAN: Investment Interaction

Like trade, foreign investment during 1980s and 1990s played important role in shaping rapid economic development of the ASEAN-5. Until China arrived on the map of world FDI, the ASEAN-5, especially Singapore, were the most favourable investment destination among developing countries. Even after China's graduation as most friendly FDI host country the ASEAN-5 continued to receive respectable share in world FDI inflows. Among principal attractions of ASEAN-5 were rapid industrialization, export orientation, policy of openness, progressive and positive attitude towards foreign investment.

Contrary to ASEAN-5 positive perception about foreign investment and its catalyst role in economic development, India until lately 1991 was least curious towards FDI and involved in conflicting discussion concerning opening the economy to foreign investors. It does not imply that there were no foreign investments in the economy before 1991 but no definite policy drive to make India as a favourite investment destination. Till 1991 the amount of foreign investment was hardly noticeable in the economy. What was the fall-out of apathy towards FDI? The economy was invisible on world investment scene even though in her neighbourhood (i.e. in ASEAN-5 and China) FDI was playing miracle in changing their economic scenario.

The Table: 4.1 gives the comparative picture of significance of FDI in activating domestic investment in ASEAN-5 and India. During 1986-91 the share of inward FDI flows to gross capital formation in ASEAN-5 was 13.3 per cent; and share of outward FDI flows to gross capital formation was 2 per cent. These percentages were quite remarkable in the world and much higher than the percentage of other developing countries including China. For India, the same corresponding figures for the period were 0.3 per cent and zero.

During 1992-97 in case of ASEAN-5 the share of inward FDI flows to capital formation marginally descended to 11.8 per cent while that of outward FDI flows to capital formation increased to 4.3 per cent indicating that these countries were in a position to source out sizeable FDI amount to the outside world. The relative decrease in ASEAN-5 FDI inflows in 1990s may be owing to two reasons: First the "flying geese" pattern of FDI worked in favour of China after staying over for a considerable period in ASEAN-5, and second along with China, other developing countries outside Asia region emerged as "favourable host" to FDI diverting foreign investment of developed countries there instead ASEAN-5. India's figures during 1992-97 got marginally improved but certainly nowhere near to ASEAN-5. The high proportion of inward FDI flows to capital formation in ASEAN-5 and China points towards effectiveness of FDI in their economic development.[1]

In this chapter we would discuss (i) overall FDI inflows in India and share of ASEAN-5 in it; (ii) two-way investment transactions between India and ASEAN-5; (iii) future potentials (iv) emerging trend in investment interaction between India and ASEAN-5.

Overall FDI inflows in India and Share of ASEAN-5

We would begin with examining the extent and role of ASEAN-5 FDI in Indian economy and the pattern of FDI from all investing countries in India. One thing is essentially noticeable in the case of India is that share of FDI (compared to portfolio investment) in total investment is steadily growing up since 1994-95 and in the last two years (i.e. 1997-98 and 1998-99) it has overtaken to portfolio investment. Rather in 1998-99 the portfolio investment has registered negative share in total investment because of large-scale withdrawal by FIIs in the aftermath of the Asian crisis. The rising share of FDI in total investment could be seen as an indicator of burgeoning confidence of foreign investors to invest their money for a longer period and it also signifies the soundness of macro-economic fundamentals of India [see Table: 4.2].

The Tables 4.3(a) and 4.3(b) show the aggregate FDI flows from top 10 investing countries into India between 1992-99. The relative insignificance of ASEAN investment is most conspicuous. Only Singapore, among the ASEAN-5 is marginally significant in investing in India; while investments from Malaysia, Indonesia, Thailand and Philippines are considered relatively negligible to be lumped together under the residual category of "others". Even the Singapore's FDI flows can not be counted as "major" investment given its small share in India's total investment (about 2 per cent) and in value terms about US $ 25 million annually.

Given the Singapore's huge aggregate FDI outflows about US$4.1 billion annually India's share in it is just 0.6 per cent. Singapore's major chunk of FDI outflows goes to China for obvious reasons. Singapore's comparative advantage in the areas of construction, light industry manufacturing, and beverage and food processing find suitable partners in China. The small and medium-sized Singapore firms are actively involved in FDI in China where on the basis of their ethnic ties they get dialect advantage. Singapore's managerial expertise and "software" in property development, industrial park construction, doing business with multinational corporations, and handling technology transfers are in high demand in China. Besides, both ethnic ties and governmental encouragement have favoured and influenced business ventures between Singapore and China.[2]

The countries dominating FDI scene in India are USA, Japan, Germany, S. Korea and Netherlands. During 1992-99 the annual share of USA in India's total FDI is 19 per cent (US$271 million); Japan's share is 7 per cent (US$102 million); Germany's 6 per cent (US$89 million) and South Korea's and Netherlands' is 5 per cent each. Mauritius though tops the list of investors with 31 per cent share in total investment however its foreign investment does not originate from that country. The foreign investors of other countries mostly use Mauritius primarily as an off shore financial centre to channelise their investments to gain certain benefits offered by India to Mauritius. A large no. of Mauritian population is of Indian ethnic and India has age-old and intimate cultural ties with Mauritius.

Among various sectors where FDI are largely attracted in India are engineering followed by chemicals of allied products, electronics and electrical equipment, etc. The average share of FDI in engineering activity during 1992-98 is 22 per cent; and that of chemicals and allied products and electronics and electrical equipment is 13 per cent each. The shares of other two sectors; namely finance and services are 10 and 9 per cent respectively [see Table: 4:4(a) and 4.4(b)].

ASEAN-5 Investment in India

On the basis of number of investment approval, the cumulative ASEAN-5 no. of FDI and technology agreements in India during 1991-2000 are 866, i.e. about 4.6 per cent of total agreements which India entered with all other countries. Out of these 866, 542 are financial and 324 are technical agreements. Singapore's share among ASEAN-5 total agreements (with India) is about 65 per cent, followed by Malaysia 17 per cent and Thailand with 12 per cent. Philippines' and Indonesia's share in these approvals are 5 and 2 per cent respectively [see Table: 4.5]. On the basis of approved FDI value Malaysia's contribution is Rupees 56 billion and tops the list among ASEAN-5. Singapore's investment is Rupees 45 billion; Thailand's about Rupees 25 billion and that of Indonesia and Philippines is about Rupees 4 billion each.[3] The aggregate share of ASEAN-5 in India's total approved FDI value is 5 per cent [See Table: 4.6].

The above data further highlights the relative insignificance of ASEAN-5 investments in India in both financial and technical sectors. The trend of rapid growth of ASEAN-5 investment in India's financial sector is commensurate with similar sort of tendency displayed by other major investors such as USA, Netherlands, UK and France. However, these developed countries' investors have manifested equal interest in India's technical sector too. The investors from Germany, Japan and Italy have rather demonstrated more inclination towards technical sector. Among ASEAN-5, investors from Singapore, Malaysia and Thailand mostly prefer India's financial sector even though large opportunities are possible in technical sector [see Table : 4.7].

Indian Investment in ASEAN-5

As pointed out earlier here India's overall FDI outflows is hardly noticeable during the entire period, i.e. 1985-98. To make it clear, in 1986-91 the annual FDI outflows is US$3 million and in 1992-98 it is US $ 85 million. If we compare these figures with ASEAN-5 then we notice glaring difference between India and ASEAN-5 in outflowing FDI. The corresponding figures of ASEAN-5 in 1986-91 is US$1.1 billion annually and rose to US$7 billion in 1992-98.[4] The abysmally low amount of India's overall FDI outflows is reflected in absolutely insignificant presence of Indian investment in ASEAN-5.

The Table: 4.8 gives the overall picture of Indian joint ventures and wholly owned subsidiaries until 1995 on approval basis. On the basis of equity amount, the West Asia region with 37 per cent share leads in hosting Indian joint ventures. Next is Europe with 18 per cent share and ASEAN-5 share is 12 per cent in equity. Among ASEAN-5, Malaysia hosts largest no. of Indian joint ventures i.e. 39, followed by Singapore with 37. But on the basis of equity amount, Indonesia and Thailand are much ahead of Singapore in hosting Indian investment. On the front of wholly owned subsidiaries Europe is a leading region to have 152 Indian companies with 48 per cent share in total equity investment. Singapore leads the tally among ASEAN-5 with 56 companies with substantial share in equity amount. Philippines does not have any Indian subsidiary and the other three countries namely, Indonesia, Malaysia and Thailand together have only 10 companies indicating that only Singapore from the region is hosting majority of Indian subsidiaries.

Almost the similar sort of trend regarding Indian joint ventures and wholly owned subsidiaries (of 1995) continued to during 1996 and 1997. The Table: 4.9 depicts that West Asia, Europe, America and Africa region continues to be important in having sizeable no. of Indian joint ventures while ASEAN-5 remained relatively less important. Relatedly, in case of Indian wholly owned subsidiaries the Europe dominates the scene by holding 91 companies with about 43 per cent share in total equity investment. The other regions which host substantial amount of equity are West Asia, Africa and America. The share of ASEAN-5 in Indian equity is below 10 per cent.

The foregoing scenario much altered during 1998 to 2000 when Indian entrepreneurs from information technology (IT) sector rushed to establish joint ventures in US. The open invitation and encouragement to Indian IT entrepreneurs to start their businesses in Silicon Valley of US facilitated large FDI outflow to US. Correspondingly the share of ASEAN-5 in Indian FDI outflow much reduced during the same period. Even the Indian FDI share in their wholly owned subsidiaries in US has substantially increased and that of ASEAN-5 gone down. However, the Europe continued to hold largest chunk of Indian FDI outflow during the period. Indian investment in ASEAN-5 is mostly concentrated in activities related to services sector such as development of computer software, electronic services, hotel industry, professional managerial and engineering training and consultancy (See Table: 4.10).

Future Investment Potential

Presently ASEAN-5 investment in India is concentrated in few areas such as financial services, development of express ways/national highways, food processing, palm oil ventures, etc. The ASEAN-5 competitive advantage lies in manufacturing activity in small and medium-sized enterprises. For ASEAN-5 investors, restrictions on maximum level of foreign equity in India's small scale sector goes against their investment interest. The maximum limit is 24 per cent equity to foreign investors in India's small scale sector. In contrast, China has kept minimum level of foreign equity at 25 per cent. This provision makes China's small scale sector more attractive than India and ASEAN-5 investors, particularly from Singapore prefer to invest in China.

To make the economy more attractive to private and foreign investors the Indian Govt. on May 10, 2001 made following announcement: 100 per cent foreign equity will be allowed in drugs and pharmaceutical industry, air ports, township development, hotel and tourism, courier service, and mass rapid transport system (MRTS). Further the limit of foreign equity in telecom sector is raised to 74 from 49 per cent. Similarly foreign equity in banks is hiked to 49 from 20 per cent. Besides defence production is opened up to private sector and private equity up to 26 per cent will be allowed in production of defence equipment.

In the light of various recent changes announced by the Indian Govt. we would identify thrust areas where both India and ASEAN-5 can enhance their two-way investment cooperation.

Indonesia

For Indonesian investors the following Indian sectors could be potential areas: ports—inland ports and waterways sector; oil refining sector; manufacturing activity in special economic zones (SEZs); electricity generation, transmission and distribution (other than atomic reactor plants). Indonesia possesses expertise in port construction and development and this can be utilised in development of Indian ports. Recently the Indian Govt. has announced 10 year tax holiday for investment in ports sector plus tax incentive for providing long-term finance or investment in equity capital of the enterprise engaged in development of port infrastructure. Any income by way of interest, dividend or long-term capital gains from such investment is fully exempt.

Similarly Indonesia possesses requisite expertise in exploration and refining of oil. For attracting FDI in oil sector the Indian Govt. has increased FDI ceiling to 100 per cent. In case of electricity generation and related activities, there is no upper limit of FDI and Indonesian expertise in this field may find right atmosphere and partner in India.

For Indian investors there are ample opportunities available in Indonesia as the latter recognises the achievement of India in developing advanced technology in the field of IT, bio-informatics, genetic engineering, agro-based production, etc. The following could be potential areas for Indian investors: IT sector, pharmaceutical and health care sector, machine tools and accessories, textile machinery, dyes and dye intermediates, refining of used lubricants, rubber products, heavy electrical machinery, agricultural plantation in coconut, cocoa, coffee, soybean, corn and potato, shrimp farming, automotive components. The Indonesian IT sector could be an immediate attraction for Indian investors and the Indian Govt. has now facilitated overseas investment by announcing that the Indian company can invest up to US$ 50 million abroad annually through the automatic route without being subjected to the 3 year profitability condition.

Malaysia

For Malaysian investors India's infrastructure sector especially construction and development of expressways/ national highways would continue to be attractive. Recently the Indian government announced 100 per cent foreign unity in mass rapid transport system (MRTS). Besides, Malaysian investors can bring in their expertise in airports, township development, hotel and tourism industry as these sectors are now fully opened up to foreign equity. Further development and expansion of marine ports at various places could be another area for Malaysian investors.

Malaysia offers more liberal investment regime to foreign investors. Already Indian entrepreneurs have established either joint ventures or wholly owned subsidiaries there in the areas of palm oil refining, drugs and pharmaceuticals, insurance, textiles and yarn manufacturing, automobile associated activities, etc. The potential opportunities to Indian investors lie in health care activities including establishing medical education centre plus hospitals, production of generic and other drugs. In addition Indian investors can diversify their investment in resource-based industries such as palm oil, timber, petroleum and rubber.

Philippines

India's investment interaction with Philippines and vice-versa is not as strong as it is with other ASEAN-5 countries. So far no Indian investor has ever invested in Philippines but Filipino investors have invested in India's drugs and pharmaceutical industry. There are no apparent reasons for their lower investment cooperation, nevertheless it could be related to their lower trade interaction. Over the years Philippines has acquired excellence in developing advanced Information and Communication Technology (ICT) sector and Indian investors can tie up with Filipino entrepreneurs to market computer software in Asia-Pacific region.

Singapore

Singapore's investment is relatively large and spread in various activities in India such as service sectors, infrastructure projects like telecom, IT products, development of industrial and electronic parks, joint ventures in non-banking financial companies (NBFCs), etc. In coming days the Singapore investors can avail the advantage of further opening of certain sectors for 100 per cent foreign equity such as drugs and pharmaceuticals, air ports, township development, and mass rapid transport system (MRTS). In addition they can tap new opportunities thrown open in bank and defence production sector. Given the Singapore investors' expertise and large investment capability India would expect that they should take up such projects where advanced technical knowhow plus large investment is required. Such projects would be participation in disinvestment of Videsh Sanchar Nigam Ltd. (VSNL), Air India and Maruti Udyog Ltd. Recently the Port of Singapore Authority (PSA) has carried out feasible study to work on port project in Gujarat, Tuticorin in Tamil Nadu and Nhava-Sheva port in Mumbai.

Indian investors have already marked their presence in various sectors in Singapore such as consultancy services, trading in agro-based products, software development services, electronic equipments, family and media entertainment, shipping, etc. Singapore expects that Indian investors should come in big way especially in shipping activity because India possesses necessary technical knowhow in this activity. Other promising area is exploration of oil and petroleum material. Recently Singapore High Commissioner in India has urged Indian business community to explore the emerging opportunities of setting up front-end marketing outfits in Singapore for third country exports. This would help Indian traders to enhance their exports to neighbouring Asia-Pacific countries.

The Indian investors can take advantage of the recent announcement by the Indian Govt. with regard to enhancement of investment limit up to US$ 50 million abroad annually without being subjected to the 3 years profitability condition. Another related new announcement is that the companies which have issued ADRs/GDRs may acquire shares of foreign companies up to US$ 100 million or an amount equivalent to ten times the value of their exports in a year, which ever is higher. Indian investors, particularly in Singapore's IT sector can take advantage of these provisions.

Thailand

Thai investors so far invested in limited activities in India. Their investment is largely concentrated in agro-based industry, manufacturing of agricultural related machinery, marine products, pharmaceutical industry. India offers opportunities in agriculture resource-based industry, tourism, deep-sea fishing, pharmaceutical, health care. The point to note here is that currently Thai economy is in process of restructuring (in the backdrop of financial crisis) and therefore its investors may not be ready to take risk beyond ASEAN region boundary.

Indian investors in Thailand have invested in certain activities such as chemical products, engineering and financial consultancy, metallurgical production, pharmaceutical chemicals, paper and paper products, etc. As regards future potential it could be in health-care products; establishing training and education centres in medical sciences, computer software, engineering sciences; tourism and hotel industry; agro-based products; manufacturing of machinery required for small scale industry.

Emerging Trend

The ongoing level of two-way investment cooperation may not sound encouraging to both the sides mainly because India on her part can not step up large-scale investment in ASEAN-5 in immediate future unless the investors link up their investment with export of merchandise goods and services. It underlines the fact that wherever in the world investment grows up it travels to earn long term benefits of trade in goods and services. It happened in the case of USA, Japan and other developed countries and it is happening with developing countries including ASEAN-5 too. The example cited in this connection here is Singapore's FDI in China. Singaporean small firms are investing in Chinese firms to reap the advantages of China's large market. For Indian manufacturers the indigenous market is not only huge but relatively much protected for local products which pays adequate returns to them. To enhance Indian investment in ASEAN-5 the manufacturers would need to identify products which they can produce at comparatively low cost in ASEAN-5 and market them in ASEAN countries.[5] Right now there are no such serious attempts and Indian investors have looked upon ASEAN-5 as destination for investment in services sector such as computer software, electronic services, hotel industry, professional managerial and engineering training, consultancy etc.

For attracting ASEAN-5 investment in India there is urgent need to open local market for consumer products of ASEAN-5. Presently ASEAN-5 investment in India's manufacturing sector is at low level and more in services sector. India would prefer ASEAN-5 investment get attracted in manufacturing sector because along with FDI ASEAN technology may get transferred and help India to enhance her competitive edge in producing quality products. For ASEAN-5 investors, restrictions on maximum level of foreign equity in India's small scale sector goes against their investment interest. The maximum limit is 24 per cent equity to foreign investors in India's small scale sector. In contrast, China has kept minimum level of foreign equity at 25 per cent in its small scale sector. This provision makes China's small scale sector more attractive than India and ASEAN-5 investors, particularly Singaporean, prefer to invest in China. Of course, there are other reasons besides these concerning China's attractiveness as investment destination to ASEAN-5 investors which are already discussed here.

Table 4.1
Inward and Outward FDI flows as a percentage of gross fixed capital formation in India and ASEAN-5

(Percentage)

	1986-91 (Annual average)	*1992-97 (Annual average)*	*1992*	*1993*	*1994*	*1995*	*1996*	*1997*
World								
Inward	3.6	5.2	3.3	4.4	4.5	5.6	5.6	7.7
Outward	4.1	5.6	3.7	4.9	5.3	5.9	5.5	8.0
Developed Countries								
Inward	3.5	3.7	2.6	3.0	2.8	3.9	3.6	6.5
Outward	4.5	5.6	3.8	4.5	4.9	5.6	5.2	9.7
Developing Countries								
Inward	3.4	7.4	4.2	6.1	7.6	7.4	8.7	10.3
Outward	1.3	3.1	1.7	3.0	3.4	3.2	3.3	3.9
Asia								
Inward	2.8	6.4	3.2	6.0	7.0	6.6	7.4	8.4
Outward	1.5	3.8	2.0	3.7	4.2	4.2	4.3	4.5
ASEAN-5								
Inward	13.3	11.8	9.8	12.2	13.3	11.7	11.6	11.9
Outward	2.0	4.3	2.1	3.9	5.2	4.7	5.1	4.7
India								
Inward	0.3	2.1	0.4	1.0	1.4	2.4	2.9	4.2
Outward	Nil	0.1	Nil	Nil	0.1	0.1	0.3	0.1
China								
Inward	2.9	13.9	7.4	12.2	17.3	15.0	17.0	14.3
Outward	0.7	1.4	2.7	2.0	1.0	0.8	0.9	0.8

Source: UNCTAD' World Investment Report' relevant issues.

Table 4.2
Foreign Investment Inflows in India-Classified

(US $ Million)

	1998-99 (P)	*1997-98*	*1996-97*	*1995-96*	*1994-95*	*1993-92*	*1992-91*	*1991-92*
A) **Direct Investment**	2462	3557	2821	2133	1314	586	341	150
i) Government (SIA/FIPB)	1821	2754	1922	1249	701	280	238	87
ii) RBI	179	202	135	169	171	89	42	—
iii) NRI	62	241	639	715	442	217	61	63
iv) Acquisition of shares(1)	400	360	125	—	—	—	—	—
B) **Portfolio Investment**	-61	1828	3312	2748	3824	3649	92	08
i) GDRs(2)	270	645	1366	683	2082	1602	86	—
ii) FIIs(3)	-390	979	1926	2009	1503	1665	01	—
iii) Offshore Funds & Others	59	204	20	56	239	382	06	08
C) **TOTAL (A+B)**	2401	5385	6133	4881	5138	4235	433	158
D) Share of Direct and Portfolio investment in total foreign investment inflows(%)								
a) Direct Investment	102.5	66.1	46.0	43.7	25.57	13.84	78.75	94.94
b) Portfolio Investment	- 2.5	33.9	54.0	56.3	74.43	86.16	21.25	5.06

Notes : P-Provisional figures for 1998-99

(1) relates to acquisition of shares of Indian companies by non-resident Indian (NRIs) under section 29 of FERA. Data on such acquisition have been included as part of FDI since January 1996.

(2) represent the amount raised by Indian corporates through Global Depository Receipts.

(3) represent fresh inflow of funds by Foreign Institutional Investors.

Source : Reserve Bank of India (RBI) - 'Annual Reports' of relevant years.

Table 4.3(a)
FDI inflows in India, Country-wise distribution

(US $ Million)

Source	*1998-99*	*1997-98*	*1996-97*	*1995-96*	*1994-95*	*1993-94*	*1992-93*	*Total (annual average) 1992-93 to 1998-99*	*% sare in total*
(1) **Mauritius**	590.0	900.4	846.4	507.3	196.7	NA	NA	434.4	31
(2) **USA**	452.8	687.4	241.6	194.6	202.8	98.8	21.7	271.4	19
(3) **Japan**	235.1	163.5	96.7	60.9	94.9	36.9	25.7	102.0	07
(4) **Italy**	115.6	42.9	27.7	NA	NA	NA	NA	26.6	02
(5) **Germany**	113.5	151.4	166.2	99.7	34.6	35.1	21.4	88.8	06
(6) **South Korea**	85.3	333.1	6.3	23.9	12.0	NA	NA	65.8	05
(7) **Netherlands**	53.3	158.9	123.7	49.8	44.7	46.5	21.0	71.1	05
(8) **Singapore**	NA	NA	75.6	60.1	24.5	9.9	2.8	24.7	02
(9) **UK**	NA	NA	54.2	70.9	143.5	64.1	6.6	48.5	03
(10) **Switzerland**	NA	NA	NA	32.6	26.2	22.5	35.3	16.7	01
(11) **Others**	354.4	518.4	418.6	318.2	92.1	55.2	145.5	271.8	19
Total	2000.0	2956.0	2057.0	1418.0	872.0	369.0	280.0	1421.7	100

Note : Exclude inflows under the NRI (i.e. non resident Indian) direct investments route through the RBI and inflows due to acquisition of shares under section 29 of FERA

Source : Reserve Bank of India (RBI) - 'Annual Reports' of relevant years.

Table 4.3(b)
FDI inflows in India, Country-wise distribution

(Rupees Crore)

Source	*1998-99*	*1997-98*	*1996-97*	*1995-96*	*1994-95*	*1993-94*	*1992-93*
(1) **Mauritius**	2482.2	3346.3	3004.7	1697.0	617.7	NA	NA
(2) **USA**	1904.9	2554.7	857.6	650.9	636.9	309.9	66.4
(3) **Japan**	989.0	607.5	343.3	203.8	298.1	115.7	78.9
(4) **Italy**	486.3	159.6	98.4	NA	NA	NA	NA
(5) **Germany**	477.7	562.6	589.9	333.6	108.5	110.0	65.6
(6) **South Korea**	358.7	1238.0	22.2	79.9	37.6	NA	NA
(7) **Netherlands**	224.2	590.5	439.3	166.7	140.2	145.8	64.5
(8) **Singapore**	NA	NA	268.4	201.1	76.8	30.9	08.6
(9) **UK**	NA	NA	192.4	237.1	450.5	201	20.2
(10) **Switzerland**	NA	NA	NA	111.4	82.3	70.7	108.3
(11) **Others**	1491.3	1926.6	1495.8	1061.5	289.4	173.3	445.7
Total	8414.3	10985.9	7312.0	4743.0	2738.0	1157.3	858.2

Note: Exclude inflows under the NRI (i.e. non resident Indian) direct investments route through the RBI and inflows due to acquisition of shares under section 29 of FERA

Source: Reserve Bank of India (RBI), 'Annual Reports' of relevant years.

Table 4.4(a)
Foreign Investment in India, Industry-wise classified

(US $ Million)

Source	*1998-99*	*1997-98*	*1996-97*	*1995-96*	*1994-95*	*1993-94*	*1992-93*	*Total (annual average) 1992-93 to 1998-99*	*% sare in total*
(1) **Engineering**	427.6	579.9	730.2	251.9	131.6	32.9	69.8	318	22
(2) **Chemicals &** Allied Products	375.5	257.3	303.8	126.7	141.2	37.5	47.0	184	13
(3) **Services**	368.5	321.3	15.2	100.4	93.4	20.2	2.4	132	09
(4) **Electronics &** Electrical Equipment	228.3	644.6	153.6	129.6	56.4	57.1	32.8	186	13
(5) **Finance**	184.8	147.9	217.0	270.0	97.7	42.2	3.7	138	10
(6) **Computers**	106.2	139.2	58.7	52.1	10.2	7.6	8.3	55	04
(7) **Pharmaceuticals**	28.4	33.8	47.6	54.8	10.1	49.5	3.1	33	02
(8) **Food & Diary** Products	18.6	112.3	237.5	85.0	60.9	43.5	27.9	84	06
(9) **Others**	262.1	719.7	293.4	347.5	270.5	78.5	85.0	294	21
Total	2000.0	2956.0	2057.0	1418.0	872.0	369.0	280.0	1422	100

Note: Exclude inflows under the NRI (i.e. non resident Indian) direct investments route through the RBI and inflows due to acquisition of shares under section 29 of FERA

Source: Reserve Bank of India (RBI), 'Annual Reports' of relevant years.

Table 4.4(b)
Foreign Investment in India, Industry-wise classified

(Rupees Crore)

Source	*1998-99*	*1997-98*	*1996-97*	*1995-96*	*1994-95*	*1993-94*	*1992-93*
(1) **Engineering**	1799.1	2155.2	2592.2	842.5	413.2	103.1	214.0
(2) **Chemicals &** Allied Products	1579.9	956.2	1078.5	423.8	443.3	117.5	144.1
(3) **Services**	1550.3	1194.1	53.9	336.0	293.2	63.3	7.5
(4) **Electronics &** Electrical Equipment	960.4	2395.6	545.4	433.6	177.1	179.2	100.5
(5) **Finance**	777.6	549.7	770.4	903.3	306.9	132.3	11.3
(6) **Computers**	446.7	517.2	208.4	174.3	32.0	23.9	25.3
(7) **Pharmaceuticals**	119.6	125.6	169.0	183.2	31.7	155.3	9.6
(8) **Food & Diary** Products	78.1	417.8	843.2	284.2	191.3	136.5	85.5
(9) **Others**	1102.8	2674.6	1051.0	1162.1	849.3	246.2	260.4
Total	8414.3	10985.9	7312.0	4743.0	2738.0	1157.3	858.2

Source : RBI 'Annual Reports' relevant issues.

Table 4.5
ASEAN-5 FDI and Foreign Technology Agreements with India (Total of approvals during 1991 to 2000)

Rank No.	*Countries*	*No. of Approval*			*Percent of Total Approval*
		Total	*Finance*	*Technology*	
1.	Singapore	560	341	219	3.0
2.	Malaysia	148	102	46	0.78
3.	Thailand	103	68	35	0.54
4.	Philippines	41	21	20	0.22
5.	Indonesia	14	10	04	0.07
	Total of ASEAN-5	866	542	324	4.58
	Total of All countries including above	18919	12050	6869	

Source: Secretariat for Industrial Assistance, Govt. of India, *SIA Newsletter* relevant issues.

Table 4.6
ASEAN-5 FDI in India
(Total of value of approvals during 1991 to 2000)

(Amount in Indian Rupees Billion)

Rank No.	*Countries*	*FDI Value (Rupees)*	*Percent of Total*
1.	Malaysia	55.77	2.26
2.	Singapore	44.83	1.82
3.	Thailand	24.59	1.00
4.	Indonesia	3.93	0.16
5.	Philippines	3.85	0.15
	Total of ASEAN-5	132.97	5.39
	Total of All countries including above	2467.90	

Source: Secretariat for Industrial Assistance, Govt. of India, *SIA Newsletter* relevant issues.

Table 4.7
Top 10 Country sources of FDI and Foreign Technology Agreements in India
(Cumulative total of approvals during 1991 to 2000)

Rank No.	*Countries*	*Nó. of Approval*			*Percent of Total Approval*
		Total	*Finance*	*Technology*	
1.	USA	3882	2417	1465	20.5
2.	Germany	2116	1104	1012	11.25
3.	United Kingdom	1813	1033	780	9.6
4.	Japan	1259	551	708	6.7
5.	Netherlands	901	610	291	4.8
6.	Italy	839	408	431	4.4
7.	Mauritius	773	742	31	4.1
8.	France	682	401	281	3.6
9.	Switzerland	673	388	285	3.6
10.	Singapore	560	341	219	3.0
	Total of (1 to 10)	13498	8111	5387	71.3
	Total of All countries including above	18919	12050	6869	100.0

Source: Secretariat for Industrial Assistance, Govt. of India, '*SIA Newsletter*' relevant issues.

Table 4.8

Indian Joint Ventures & Wholly Owned Subsidiaries Abroad Approved upto 31st December, 1995

(Equity in lakhs of Rupees)

Region	*Joint Ventures*		*% share in Equity Total*	*Wholly Owned Subsidiaries*		*% share in Equity Total*
	No.	*Equity*		*No.*	*Equity*	
Africa	55	9246.22	5.2	45	17668.60	11.1
America	58	26681.16	15.0	105	15685.24	9.9
East Asia	141	25304.69	14.3	91	42078.50	26.6
Indonesia	18	6779.54		02	2.09	
Malaysia	39	8721.75		06	829.90	
Philippines	01	135.31	12.2	—	—	16.6
Singapore	37	1915.53		56	25486.26	
Thailand	24	4162.64		02	50.60	
Europe	164	32190.50	18.2	152	75483.23	47.8
Oceania	14	2727.68	1.6	0.	1079.53	0.007
South Asia	83	15197.47	8.6	16	5270.44	3.3
West Asia	78	66199.93	37.3	11	1385.29	0.009
Total	593	177547.65	100.0	423	158650.83	100.0

Source: Indian Investment Centre, *Monthly Newsletter*, various relevant issues.

Table 4.9
Indian Joint Ventures & Wholly Owned Subsidiaries Abroad Approved during 1996 and 1997

(Equity in US $'000)

Region	*Joint Ventures*		*% share in Equity Total*	*Wholly Owned Subsidiaries*		*% share in Equity Total*
	No.	*Equity*		*No.*	*Equity*	
Africa	26	58765	13.1	34	42559	14.7
America	37	68031	15.1	77	36094	12.5
East Asia	39	28765	6.4	44	25464	8.8
Indonesia	03	898		01	500	
Malaysia	13	1272		03	3800	
Singapore	10	13980	4.9		16774	7.3
Thailand	05	5696		—	—	
Europe	51	122419	27.2	91	123649	42.7
Oceania	04	244	0.5	02	135	0.0005
South Asia	35	29283	6.5	09	8396	2.9
West Asia	22	142850	31.7	11	53034	18.3
Total	214	450357	100.0	268	289331	100.0

Source: Indian Investment Centre, *Monthly Newsletter* various relevant issues.

Table 4.10
Indian Joint Ventures & Wholly Owned Subsidiaries Abroad Approved during 1998 and 2000

(Equity in US $'000)

Region	*Joint Ventures*		*% share in Equity Total*	*Wholly Owned Subsidiaries*		*% share in Equity Total*
	No.	*Equity*		*No.*	*Equity*	
Africa	38	42159.1	5.02	100	190450.90	12.4
America	112	257303.31	30.7	364	627374.30	40.1
East Asia	53	35477.60	4.2	92	45157.90	2.9
Indonesia	02	1097.00	} 4.0	02	508.50	} 1.2
Malaysia	09	7604.30		07	208.40	
Philippines	Nil	Nil		Nil	Nil	
Singapore	16	5106.40		56	16917.9	
Thailand	08	16337.30		01	10.0	
Europe	94	373866.40	44.5	187	609602.3	39.7
Oceania	05	1197.7	0.14	14	9971.7	0.65
South Asia	50	23341.7	2.8	35	42297.7	2.8
West Asia	53	94768.0	11.3	27	9301.3	0.61
Grand Total	408	839413.81	100.0	819	1534156.1	100.0

Source: Indian Investment Centre *Monthly Newsletter* various relevant issues.

Note: In year 2000 one joint venture with capital US $ 10,500 was established in CIS and it is included here in Grand Total.

Table 4.A

Inward and Outward FDI flows as a percentage of gross fixed capital formation in ASEAN-5

(Percentage)

	1986-91 (Annual average)	*1992-97 (Annual average)*	*1992*	*1993*	*1994*	*1995*	*1996*	*1997*
Malaysia								
Inward	14.7	15.9	26.0	20.3	14.9	11.0	11.1	12.2
Outward	2.9	6.4	2.6	5.4	6.2	6.9	8.8	8.2
Philippines								
Inward	6.6	7.5	2.1	9.6	10.5	8.9	7.8	6.1
Outward	Nil	1.2	Nil	2.9	2.0	0.6	0.9	0.7
Singapore								
Inward	37.6	25.7	12.4	23.0	35.0	28.9	27.5	27.3
Outward	6.9	12.4	7.4	9.9	15.7	14.0	14.0	13.3
Thailand								
Inward	5.5	3.9	4.8	3.6	2.3	2.9	3.0	6.8
Outward	0.4	0.8	0.3	0.5	0.9	1.3	1.2	0.8
Indonesia								
Inward	2.3	5.7	3.9	4.3	3.8	6.7	8.5	7.0
Outward	Nil	0.7	0.1	0.8	1.1	0.9	0.7	0.3

Source: UNCTAD' World Investment Report' relevant issues.

Table 4.B
FDI Outflows of ASEAN, 1986-98

(USS Million)

	1986-91 (Annual average)	*1992-98 (Annual average)*	*1992*	*1993*	*1994*	*1995*	*1996*	*1997*	*1998*
ASEAN	1067	7566	2035	4631	8572	11281	12160	8918	5365
ASEAN-5	1067	7548	2035	4579	8572	11260	12120	8908	5355
Indonesia	07	349	52	356	609	603	600	178	44
Malaysia	311	2448	514	1464	2591	3091	4133	3425	1921
Philippines	–1	223	05	374	302	399	182	136	160
Singapore	658	4062	1317	2152	4577	6281	6274	4722	3108
Thailand	92	466	147	233	493	886	931	447	122
Brunei	Nil	18	Nil	50	NA	20	40	10	10
Cambodia	Nil	0.3	Nil	02	NA	NA	NA	NA	NA
Laos	Nil	Nil	Nil	Nil	Nil	Nil	Nil	Nil	Nil
Myanmar	Nil	Nil	Nil	Nil	Nil	Nil	Nil	Nil	Nil
Vietnam	Nil	0.1	Nil	Nil	NA	01	NA	NA	NA

Source: UNCTAD' World Investment Report' relevant issues.

Table 4.C
FDI Inflows of ASEAN, 1986-98

(USS Million)

	1986-91 (Annual average)	1992-98 (Annual average)	1992	1993	1994	1995	1996	1997	1998
ASEAN	7908	20694	12107	15508	18699	22519	26813	27813	21400
ASEAN-5	7769	18847	11506	14738	17732	20151	24094	24444	19271
Indonesia	746	2964	1777	2004	2109	4348	6194	4673	–356
Malaysia	1605	4595	5183	5006	4342	4132	4672	5106	3727
Philippines	501	1282	228	1238	1591	1459	1520	1222	1713
Singapore	3592	7119	2204	4686	8368	8210	9440	9710	7218
Thailand	1325	2887	2114	1804	1322	2002	2268	3733	6969
Brunei	NA	07	04	14	06	07	09	05	04
Cambodia	NA	135	33	54	69	151	294	204	140
Laos	03	69	08	30	59	95	160	86	45
Myanmar	68	113	171	149	91	115	100	124	40
Vietnam	68	1522	385	523	742	2000	2156	2950	1900

Source: UNCTAD' World Investment Report', relevant issues.

Annexure 4.D
Approvals for ASEAN- 5 FDI and Foreign Technology Agreements in India—1991 to 2000

(No of Approvals)

	1991			1992			1993			1994		
Name of Country	*Total*	*Fin.*	*Tech*	*Total*	*Fin.*	*Tech*	*Total*	*Fin.*	*Tech*	*Total*	*Fin.*	*Tech*
Indonesia	0	0	0	3	3	0	2	1	1	1	0	1
Malaysia	2	1	1	3	1	2	8	5	3	11	9	2
Philippines	0	0	0	3	1	2	6	6	0	8	2	6
Singapore	7	2	5	36	24	12	41	28	13	64	45	19
Thailand	0	0	0	7	4	3	8	4	4	20	10	10
Total of ASEAN-5	9	3	6	52	33	19	65	44	21	104	66	38
Total of All Countries including above	950	289	661	1520	692	828	1476	785	691	1854	1062	792
% share of ASEAN-5 in total	0.95			3.4			4.4			5.6		
	1995			*1996*			*1997*			*1998*		
Indonesia	2	2	0	2	2	0	1	1	0	1	1	0
Malaysia	20	18	2	15	14	1	39	37	2	13	12	1
Philippines	16	6	10	5	5	0	1	1	0	0	0	0

Contd....

Annexure 4.D (contd.)

	1995			*1996*			*1997*			*1998*		
Name of Country	*Total*	*Fin.*	*Tech*	*Total*	*Fin.*	*Tech*	*Total*	*Fin.*	*Tech*	*Total*	*Fin.*	*Tech*
Singapore	65	56	9	66	58	8	86	74	12	51	40	11
Thailand	15	13	2	22	18	4	9	8	1	6	4	2
Total of ASEAN-5	118	95	23	110	97	13	136	121	15	71	57	14
Total of All Countries including above	2337	1355	982	2303	1559	744	2325	1665	660	1786	1191	595
% share of ASEAN-5 in total	5.0			4.8			5.8			4.0		
	1999			*2000*								
Indonesia	0	0	0	02	02	00						
Malaysia	20	17	03	17	15	02						
Philippines	0	0	0	02	02	00						
Singapore	70	64	06	74	66	08						
Thailand	09	07	02	07	02	05						
Total of ASEAN-5	99	88	11	102	87	15						
Total of All Countries including above	2224	1726	498	2144	1726	418						
% share of Asean-5 in total	4.5			4.8								

Source: Secretariat for Industrial Assistance, Govt. of India *SIA Newsletter* relevant issues.

ANNEXURE : 4.E

Top 10 Country Sources of FDI (Approval) Amount
(Cumulative total of value during 1991 to 2000)

(Rupees in Billion)

Rank No.	*Country*	*FDI value (Amount)*	*Percent in Total*	*Rank No.*	*Country*	*FDI Value (Amount)*	*Percent in No.*
1.	USA	472.60	19.15	6	Australia	71.56	2.90
2.	Mauritius	276.24	11.19	7	Malaysia	55.77	2.26
3.	UK	163.88	6.64	8	Israel	51.02	2.06
4.	Japan	92.72	3.76	9	Netherlands	46.13	1.87
5.	Germany	84.97	3.44	10	France	20.10	0.81
					Total of All countries including Above (in Rupees)	2467.9	
					% share of these top 10 countries in total FDI value	54.09	

Source: Secretariat for Industrial Assistance, Govt. of India *SIA Newsletter*, relevant issues.

NOTES & REFERENCES

1 For country-wise yearly classified data concerning proportion of 'inward and upward FDI flows in ASEAN-5, See Annexure: 4 A.

2 Ding Lu and Zhu Gangti (1996), "Singapore FDI in China-Features and Implications" in *ASEAN Economic Bulletin*, Singapore, Vol. 12, No. 1, pp. 53-63.

3 For detailed and classified country-wise data on total approvals from ASEAN-5, See Annexure: 4 D and 4 E.

4 For classified data about FDI outflows and inflows about ASEAN countries, see Annexure : 4 B and 4 C.

5. Ambatkar, Sanjay (2001), "Trends" in Foreign Investment Interaction between India and ASEAN in 1990s" in *Paradigm*, Vol. 5, No. 1.

5

AFTA: Implications for India

In the backdrop of modest trend in interaction (in trade and foreign investment) between India and ASEAN during 1985 through 2000, it would be imperative to analyse the implications of ASEAN Free Trade Area (AFTA) on India's prospects in the region.[1] Presuming that AFTA would be governed by the discriminatory trade practices, its implementation would pose serious threat to the entry of Indian exports in ASEAN market. Already for the last couple of years India's export growth rate has severely declined in general and ASEAN region in particular, it has reached to rock bottom level. The euphoria of high export growth rate of 1992-95 has much subsided in later period of 1996-99 in the backdrop of Asian financial crisis [See Table: 5.1].

Another challenge AFTA may pose is regarding slowing down of ASEAN FDI in India. Given the strong linkages between trade and investment and travelling of FDI to such destinations where trading opportunities are greater, the implementation of AFTA may prop up higher intra-region investment cooperation with the proportionate increase in intra-ASEAN trade. Currently ASEAN-5 investment in India is minuscule, about 7 per cent in total approval amount in 1990s. The utmost importance attached to the formation of AFTA is basically to enhance intra-region investment by reducing competition between the regional partners in attracting FDI from outside the region. The ASEAN countries look at AFTA as a "prime-mover" in their intra-region economic interaction and formulation of ASEAN Investment (AIA) is a step towards forging higher investment cooperation between regional states. Given the wide ranging impact of AFTA on future interaction between India and ASEAN we would analyse the issue in detail.

This chapter is organised in the following manner i) circumstances compelling ASEAN to form regional trading arrangement (RTA); ii) different forms of RTAs; iii) a brief history of various regional blocs; iv) RTAs in the context of debate on "trade creation" and "trade diversion"; v) AFTA and "trade creating" concept; vi) AFTA a "stumbling bloc" or a "building bloc"; vii) possible impact of AFTA on India and viii)could India gain from AFTA.

(i) Circumstances compelling ASEAN to form RTA

Before the World Trade Organisation (WTO) came into being on January 1, 1995 its predecessor the General Agreement on Trade and Tariff (GATT) was involved in evolving free trade among its member countries through the Uruguay Round of multilateral trade negotiations which was convened in 1986. The Uruguay Round of negotiations could not concluded until the end of 1993 and its overlong duration encouraged a number of countries to explore bilateral approaches to expanding their economic relations, by way of formation of regional trading arrangements. Secondly, the developing countries were seriously concerned about the increasing trend of bilateralism in trade relations of the major industrial countries and the uncertainty of a successful outcome of the Uruguay Round. Moreover, there was overall concern in developing countries regarding the capacity of multilateral bodies such as GATT / WTO in getting the barriers reduced to international trade and services and they felt their interests were not adequately safeguarded at the multilateral forum. Thirdly, since the beginning of 1990s many major developed countries entered into regional trade arrangements, for instance, US, Canada and Mexico formed the North American Free Trade Area (NAFTA). During the same period the European Union (EU) completed the process of formation of the European Communities' Internal Market besides signing the Maastricht Treaty to further consolidate the economic interaction between the member states of the EU.[2] These events at international level compelled the Southeast Asian nations to go for formation of regional trade area in order to protect their economic interests. Thus, at the ASEAN Summit in January 1992, at Singapore, the agreement was signed between six ASEAN nations to establish AFTA.[3]

Under the AFTA arrangement, which began in 1995, each ASEAN country would seek to reduce the level of its tariffs on imports of manufacturers as well as on highly protected categories of agriculture and other natural resource-based commodities to a range of 0 to 5 per cent by the year 2003. The plan also calls for the simultaneous elimination of non-tariff barriers to intra-ASEAN trade. The modality chosen to arrive at AFTA implementation is the Common Effective Preferential Tariff (CEPT) scheme which is a cooperative arrangement among the ASEAN members to reduce regional tariff and remove non-tariff barriers over a period starting in 1995. The 15 commodity groups were chosen to be on the fast track implying that for products having tariff greater than 20 per cent must be immediately reduced to 20 per cent; and then 0-5 per cent within 8 years.[4] For products with tariff at 20 per cent or below, tariff will be reduced to 0-5 per cent within five years. To qualify for CEPT, the goods must satisfy the ASEAN content requirement of 40 per cent referring to both single member economy and cumulative ASEAN content (See Tariff Box).

Tariff Box
Accelerated Tariff Reduction Schedule in AFTA

Normal Track	Accelerated time table
Tariffs > 20 per cent	Tariffs < 20 per cent
	0-5 per cent by 2003
20 per cent by 1998	0-5 per cent by 2000.
Fast Track	
Tariffs > 20 per cent	0-5 per cent by 2000
Tariffs < 20 per cent	0-5 per cent by 1998

The functioning of various regional arrangements such as NAFTA, AFTA, Single European Market (SEM), have created apprehensions among non-members of these groups. These regional arrangements are seen as fundamentally discriminatory in nature, contradicting the Most Favoured Nation, (MFN) principle of the WTO, which requires its members to levy tariff or other import restrictions without regard for country of origin and thereby to extend equal market access to goods from all exporting countries.[5] However, in case of AFTA, a different sets of arguments, favouring its formation, are normally put forward in terms of regional security and ASEAN's place in the Asia-Pacific region and the world. The ASEAN countries (individually and severally) during the seventies and eighties were seriously concerned about China's expansionist motive and war-like gestures towards the region. One of the ways to unify and counter China's military strength was to consolidate the region economically by attracting FDI and enhancing proportion of trade in the world.[6]

Another concern was the fear of investment diversion to neighbouring countries particularly to Northeast Asian, compelling ASEAN members to form AFTA. The ASEAN states were well-aware about rapid spread of global capitalism which was marked by a dramatic increase in the size of capital flows and a explosion in the (capital) volumes destined for developing countries. Realising the current and likely continued importance of FDI from within the East Asian region, the ASEAN leaders felt that AFTA could be used as the basis for extending guarantees to its main capital suppliers, such as Japan. To further consolidate its position on FDI, some ASEAN countries initiated the process of establishing East Asian Economic Caucus so that bilateral negotiations between ASEAN and its East Asian capital suppliers can come together to ease formalities.[7]

(ii) Different Forms of RTAs

Normally the regional arrangements fall under two broad categories: First, those that have modest aims at integration and seek only either a preferential trading arrangement (PTA), lower tariffs on imports from the (regional) partners than from the rest of the world or an Free Trade Area (FTA) - which involves zero tariffs among partners and positive, but not necessarily identical tariffs with the rest of the world, Second, those aim at "deep" integration with either a Customs Union (CU) which imposes a Common Effective Tariff (CET) by partner countries - or a Common Market as in the single market which is established by the European Community with the so called four freedoms-movements for labour, firms, services, and capital.

Types of PTAs

A PTA is any trading arrangement which permits the importation of goods from countries signatory to the PTA partner(s) at lower rates of duty than are imposed on imports from third countries. A PTA may be partial (such as 50 per cent duty reduction) or total with respect to the amount of duty reduction and with respect to the commodity coverage of the arrangement, although WTO rules require total that is zero per cent duty rates-exemption among partners.

A Free Trade Area (FTA) is a PTA in which tariff rates among members are zero, although external tariffs differ between members and are not necessarily changed as a result of PTA formation. The FTAs may cover one or more sectors or apply to all goods and services.

The Customs Union (CU) generally implies somewhat "more" integration. Generally a perfect CU must meet the following conditions:

(i) the complete elimination of tariffs as between the member territories;

(ii) the establishment of a uniform tariff on imports from outside the union;

(iii) apportionment of customs revenue between the members in accordance with an agreed formula.[8]

A common market is such in which not only movement of goods and services, but also of factors of production, relatively free among member countries. A common market normally refers to an agreement whereby countries enter into a customs union and also permit free, or at least greatly increased, mobility of factors of production among members. A single market is that in which all producers and consumers within the arrangement are governed by the same rules, in the sense that participants in one geographic part of the market may not be prevented from operating in another part of the market.

(iii) A Brief History of Various Regional Arrangements

Since the mid-nineteenth through mid twentieth century there were continued efforts, mostly in Europe, to formulate various regional arrangements in order to reduce trade barriers between European countries. These arrangements were mainly of sort of customs union and could survive for short period. As that time the trade relations between various countries were not so complicated as one finds today because the trade was mostly governed by the principle of 'comparative advantage'. Naturally the objective of regional arrangements were restricted to only facilitating trade between two partners. Besides there were hardly any significant presence of foreign investment and trade was completely independent without any linkage with foreign investment. More importantly there was no onslaught of global capitalism and least influence of globalization.

The end of World War II divided the world in various political blocs and trade relations also came under the influence of changed political scenario. The post World War II period witnessed many changes at international level and three influential organizations emerged at global level, namely the World Bank, the International Monetary Fund (IMF), and the General Agreement on Trade and Tariff (GATT).

The objective of GATT was to formulate a multilateral trade body to regularize the trade rules and govern the trade by fair practices so that it could become freer and free. The GATT since its inception held several rounds of trade negotiations and attempted to reduce tariffs and non-tariff barriers to ensure free flow of trade. The impact of GATT's attempt influenced the countries across the world to liberalize trade regime and also open their economies for foreign investment.

The beginning of the process of liberalization partly led to like-minded nations to enter into regional arrangements to lower tariff and non-tariff barriers to trade. Thus came the first wave of trading arrangements during the early 1960s and it gave a major formation such as European Common Market. This wave of regionalism then spread throughout Africa, Latin America and other parts of the developing world. However, the US did not participate in any regional arrangement during this period as it was a staunch supporter of multilateralism and critical of regional groupings.[9] Regionalism then came to a halt during much of the 1970s. The second wave of regionalism started in the middle of 1980s and this time the US actively participated in regional arrangement and entered into bilateral negotiations of FTAs with Israel and Canada. But the most striking free trade agreement of US was the NAFTA with Canada and Mexico. At the same time, European integration spread with the Southern (Greece, Portugal and Spain) and the Northern enlargements (Norway and Sweden). In early 1990s the

European Community negotiated the European Agreements with Czechoslovakia, Hungary and Poland.

Likewise, throughout Africa, Asia, Latin America, and the Middle East, old arrangements were being revived and new ones were created. In Southern cone of Latin America, the Southern Common Market (MERCOSUR) came into being between Argentina, Brazil, Paraguay, and Uruguay. In South Asia, seven countries of the region namely, Bangladesh, Bhutan, India, Maldives, Nepal, Pakistan and Sri Lanka formed a regional grouping-South Asia Association for Regional Cooperation (SAARC) and decided to establish a South Asia Free Trade Area (SAFTA) by the year 2003. Currently there is hardly any nation which is not a part of one or the other regional arrangement.

The mushrooming of regional arrangements in recent period have invoked a debate concerning their emergence as threat to multilateralism and eventually to free trade. The main thrust of these arguments against regionalism is that such trading blocs, during the course of time, normally turn inward and erect high barriers against non-members. The arguments in favour of multilateralism centre around welfare improvement of world at large by giving chance to trade creation. On the contrary, trading blocs, as critics argue, lead to trade diversion and welfare of the world reduce. A question then crops up here-why do countries enter into regional arrangements? Do the geographically close countries form trading blocs to earn the advantage of lesser transportation costs of their trade? In case of EU even without the formation of FTAs or PTAs of any sort, the two EU countries trade with each other much higher than with countries from which they are far away.[10] Therefore formation of regional arrangement with EU is "natural process" and such formation can be labelled as "natural bloc". The benefits of lesser transportation costs can be seen as one of the considerations in the formation of regional bloc in EU.

However, the proximity of neighbouring countries border may not be understood as assurance in enhancing trade between such neighbouring nations. For instance, India and Pakistan share common border and are members of SAARC regional forum but their mutual trade over the past half century is at the lowest ebb. Not only that India's trade with other neighbouring countries of the region is comparatively much lower than her trade with far away countries such as Russia, US and EU. Thus, neighbourhood in international economic relations has never been a guarantee about enlarged trade nor for formation of PTAs or FTAs. In fact, the first PTA formed by the US in 1980s was with Israel which did not feature geographic proximity.[11]

(iv) Debate on "Trade Creation" and "Trade Diversion"

The whole debate on regionalism and multilateralism revolves around the central question - do regional blocs amount to trade creation or trade diversion? As noted earlier here trade creation increases world welfare whereas trade diversion causes reduction in world welfare. What is trade creation and trade diversion? We would explain it by citing an example. For instance, starting with a non-discriminatory tariff on all trading partners, the US forms a FTA with Mexico. Suppose that shoes are produced under constant costs everywhere and that the FTA results in the US importing shoes from Mexico. Is this change for the better or worse? The answer depends on who is the pre-FTA supplier of shoes. If the US produced its own shoes in the initial equilibrium, it must do so at a higher cost than Mexico. In this case, the FTA shifts shoe production from a higher - to a lower-cost source and is trade creating; welfare of the union (i.e. regional bloc) and of the world rises. If on the other hand, the US initially imports shoes from another country, say, South Korea, that country must be a lower-cost producer of shoes than Mexico. In this case, the FTA causes shoe production to shift from a lower to a higher - cost source. There is trade diversion and the welfare of the union and the world declines. In this example, trade creation is accompanied by no change in trade with the rest of the world but increased trade between partners; the world as a whole moves closer to free trade. By contrast, trade diversion is accompanied by increased trade within the union at the expense of trade with the rest of the world; national protection is extended to the regional level and the world as a whole moves away from free trade.[12]

Thus the formation of FTAs may lead to contraction of world welfare because it functions against the principle of free trade. However, there is difference between the functioning of CUs and FTAs although the impact of their existence eventually leads to trade diversion. An FTA maintains each country's individual external trade barriers but removes barriers on trade between the member countries. This may create three related consequences - first the existence of different tariff rates on the part of different member countries implies that measure must be taken to prevent 'trade deflection' (meaning the situation in which each good or service enters through the member country with the lowest tariff rate and is transshipped). This results in a need for rules of origin (ROOs) to a much greater extent than customs unions to establish that goods shipped between partners in fact originate in a partner country, because of incentives to transships from countries with lower tariff rates to those with higher ones. Secondly, although in a definitional sense it can be said that an FTA 'automatically' preserves the pre-FTA tariff level unless deliberate changes are made in tariffs and other trade barriers, ROOs can in effect 'export protection' from one partner country to an other (as for e.g., when Mexican-assembled cars are eligible for duty-free entry into US only when they consist predominately of US and Mexican or Canadian made parts, under NAFTA provisions, thus discriminating against Japanese parts producers). Thirdly, the fact that protection rates are different implies that producers in particular countries can not be facing common prices of tradables (quite aside from transport costs) or of nontradables that use significant quantities of tradables as inputs. Thus, this result yields: an

FTA can not lead to any more trade creation than can a customs union and, when ROOs export protection, an FTA leads to more trade diversion than does a customs union. Besides, FTAs may result in trade diversion through administered protection.[13] That is, if Mexican exports of a particular item should increase rapidly in US in competition with products from say, Taiwan, the US response after FTA might well be to use the administered protection remedies of anti dumping or countervailing duty relief against non-partner countries (such as Taiwan).

(v) AFTA and "trade creating" concept

A questions here arises - will AFTA lead to "trade creation" or "trade diversion"? Of course, a full-fledged AFTA will come into force from the year 2003 and initially only six countries are participating in trade liberalization process and therefore any forecast about AFTA at this stage may sound pre-mature, nevertheless, to observe its developments and set the future trends is essential. Going by the findings of some recently carried out empirical studies AFTA plan reveals that it will be mainly trade-creating because it covers wide range of traded goods and simultaneously aims at eliminating non-tariff barriers. In addition, the sectoral expansion of production and export by the ASEAN countries under the AFTA plan bears close similarity to that expected under MFN liberalization (of WTO), and the bias against agriculture and other natural resource-based sectors is reduced, although marginally.[14]

However, the AFTA plan remains essentially discriminatory in nature with regard to sectoral adjustment of consumption and imports and this raises concerns about important qualitative as well as quantitative aspects of ASEAN trade relations under AFTA. Even within the region, the liberalization of ASEAN trade limit to intrabloc trade in manufactures only and may yield generally only small improvements to economic welfare in limited ASEAN countries, such as Singapore and Malaysia (by virtue of their initially relatively open economies). Thus, the AFTA may add only marginally in world welfare. In contrast, as an alternative strategy to maximise the welfare of both ASEAN and world, an unconditional MFN liberalization policy of ASEAN trade relations with all trading partners may bring in larger gain in total ASEAN trade, because it would exploit wider differences in the sources of international comparative advantage between the ASEAN countries and their international trading partners, especially the major industrial nations.

Even ASEAN countries are aware about limited benefits of their preferential trade liberalization. There is a general feeling within the region that non-preferential tariff reduction is paurely trade creating and therefore superior than preferential trade liberalization. Moreover, the success of AFTA doesn't necessarily depend on the increases in the volume of intra-ASEAN trade it would generate. Much would depend on how the share of intra-regional trade is raised. It would be very costly for ASEAN to raise the share of intra-ASEAN trade through a combination of deep preferential tariff cuts and high external tariffs. ASEAN countries would have to pay a heavy price, were they to set a high intra-regional trade target and work at it through policy interventions. It would be better for ASEAN to go on liberalizing its trade and let the market forces determine the 'optimum' for ASEAN in terms of the ratio of intra-ASEAN trade to total trade.[15]

Then, how the success of AFTA should be measured? According to the leaders of the region, the AFTA should be judged by the increase in the volume of total trade it would generate, not by the increase in the share of intra-ASEAN trade in total trade, nor even by the increase in the volume of intra-ASEAN trade per se. ASEAN has made it explicit that the main objective of the AFTA exercise is not to increase intra-ASEAN trade but to make ASEAN products competitive internationally. Currently a few export industries of ASEAN have a significantly large presence in the world market. Only three items in all ASEAN countries have a share of more than 3 per cent share in world total trade although many items do have a high comparative advantage. The three items are wood products of Indonesia, office machinery, and communications and sound recording apparatus of Singapore.[16]

AFTA is aimed at making the region borderless, by dismantling trade barriers among member countries, in the hope that it would lead to lower production costs through efficiency gains.[17] Increase in intra-ASEAN trade is not at all the motive behind the establishment of AFTA. Because even in the absence of any regional arrangement, two ASEAN countries trade six times more than two otherwise-similar countries. The "trade-creation" with formation of AFTA will be small because of the smaller size of income of the ASEAN countries *vis-a-vis* contemporary FTAs formed by other countries.[18] ASEAN has a strong intra-regional bias over the past three decades and hence their regional trade formation can be seen as a 'natural phenomenon' instead of compulsive action.

(vi) AFTA - whether a 'Stumbling Bloc' or a 'Building Bloc'?

Based on foregoing discussion we would say that AFTA may make modest claim in terms of static impact of "trade creation". Although there is less possibility of "trade diversion" at this stage owing to strong intra-regional bias in their mutual interaction. The future of AFTA will depend upon how the regional countries, alongside trade, cooperate in other economic activities. The regional leaders look at AFTA not merely in "static terms" (i.e. trade creating) but in "dynamic terms" - i.e. generating deeper economic integration in almost all regional activities.[19] What are the dynamic impacts of regional formation? There are four possible areas which could be defined as 'dynamic' in nature and could be derived directly from regional integration: first, economies of scale; second, 'X-efficiency' improvements;

third, changes in investment flows; and fourth, the potential for industrial expansion in a developing country context.

(a) Economies of Scale

An access to expanded market could always be seen as one of the principal attractions for countries to form FTAs. A main benefit is the possibility of reaping economics of scale in production. How FTA could bring in economics of scale? In industries where production technology is characterized by decreasing costs, the domestic market alone may be too small to permit production at an optimal level. If there are high tariff walls on these goods in foreign countries, international trade might be of little or no help in allowing these firms to expand output towards the optimum. With the formation of FTA, the expanded market could present the domestic decreasing cost firms with adequate demand to produce at the optimum.

(b) X-efficiency Improvements

The term "X-efficiency" refers to the optimal organization of the productive process, for instance, work methods, incentive programmes, plant layout, management, and psychological environment at the workplace. Here we would generally refer "X-efficiency to FTA externalities relating to "technology transfer". It has been proved empirically in several studies that X-inefficiency is a far more significant cause of failure to achieve the social optimum in production than is allocative inefficiency. If inefficient practices in the workplace of a protected industry are replaced by efficient methods due to competition from the partner country, a FTA will improve productivity. This is called "forced efficiency" and represents an improvement in welfare. In addition, there may be other benefits, such as increased technology and method sharing, new ideas to stimulate the psychological atmosphere at the workplace, and increase standardization of quality and specific requirements allowing for longer production runs.

(c) Changes in Investment Flows

The formation of FTA will have several positive effects on the direction of investment flows. First, after a FTA is formed, domestic capital previously invested in partner countries in order to evade tariffs will now flow to where the return on capital is highest in the FTA. This results in a more efficient allocation of investment funds ("investment creation"). In addition, the formation of a FTA reduces the risk and uncertainty of investing in foreign countries. Secondly, the advantage of increases in FDI to a country or region are many, including the effects on technology transfer, (non-debt-creating) capital flows, and readymade markets for exports.

(d) Increase in Industrial Production

In developing countries, the nurturing of the industrial base is perceived to be of paramount importance for a number of reasons, such as self-sufficiency aspirations, workforce and social externalities, and political clout of industrialists. It implies, industrial production appears as a collective consumption good yielding a flow of satisfaction they derive directly from the consumption of industrial products. Therefore, if the country wishes to protect and expand its domestic industrial production, forming a FTA is the least expensive way of achieving such a goal (because a large market is needed to attain lower-cost production).

The AFTA convenors aim at achieving the aforesaid "dynamic gains" during the course of time. They feel AFTA would play multiple role in making the region a dynamic place wherein large scale trade and investment activities will take place. There is growing realization among member states to have consensus on major economic issues, particularly in the aftermath of 1997 financial crisis. Given the linkages and interdependence these regional countries have attained over the past-three decades, there is strong feeling that AFTA would work as a "built in stabilizer" in their interactions and therefore they look at AFTA as a "building bloc" instead a "stumbling bloc".

(vii) Possible Impact of AFTA on India

Although the ASEAN has made it clear that AFTA would practice the principle of "open regionalism," that is, extending regional liberalization to partners outside the regions however, the question remains whether this dictum would be followed in letter and spirit. The "open regionalism" demands region's efforts in both, regional as well as global liberalization. It should motivate both regional initiatives and broader multilateral negotiations in WTO. So far, ASEAN has been among the most vocal advocates of parallel regional and multilateral tracks and therefore it would be interesting to see how AFTA would work in coming days.[20]

For India, AFTA could be seen as both challenge and opportunity. Challenge in the sense that AFTA would lead to enhancing region's competitiveness in world market which may indirectly undermine India's export prospects. The ASEAN has made it clear that increase export competitiveness is one of the principal objectives of AFTA and this could be achieved by pulling together factors of production including technology. Against this background India would need to struggle hard to attain quality-wise international standards to compete with products from the ASEAN region.

Secondly, AFTA will enhance intra-ASEAN trade which has already been on rise in the backdrop of ASEAN crisis. Currently about 40 per cent of their total trade is with regional partners and for import purpose the region mostly depend upon suppliers from the industrialised countries such as USA, Japan and EU [see Table : 5.2]. Although the ASEAN convenors have made it clear that increasing intra-region trade is not the objective (of AFTA) however, the formation of trade bloc naturally enhances trade within the region and therefore AFTA could not be exception. AFTA would provide opportunity to relatively less developed countries of the region such as Mynamar, Laos, Cambodia and Vietnam to increase their trade interaction with progressive countries of the region and this would lead to higher penetration of labour-content products within the region itself.

Indian products with higher labour intensive contents may face cut-throat competition from these above mentioned four countries in the region. Because tariff rates on products from within the region would be much less as compared to the products from outside the region. India's export items such as, cotton and other ready-made textile garments, may suffer severe set back in the ASEAN market with the expansion and subsequent inclusion of above mentioned four countries in AFTA. Besides the operationalization of AFTA may bring in force the 'rule of origin' against the exports originating outside from the region and this may further jeoparadise India's export interests in the region.

Thirdly, AFTA would slow down ASEAN foreign investment in India mainly because ASEAN investors link their investment with trading opportunities. The ASEAN investors hold the views that Indian consumer (product) market is still highly protected and wide opening of the market is not in sight. The implementation of AFTA would ensure higher trade interaction between the regional partners which would eventually lead to higher investment opportunities between them. Especially the affluent economies of the region would tap relatively less developed economies of the region to reap the benefit of low labour cost plus abundant natural resources[21] Obviously India would get neglected in the process and suffer in long term. Already for ASEAN investors India is not a favourable investment destination and AFTA would certainly help these investors to concentrate on regional countries, instead going outside the regional boundary.

Against the aforesaid challenges India would have to search opportunities as creation of AFTA is reality and India would have to cope with the situation. Despite a lack of commonality there is growing trade cooperation, although of moderate magnitude, between India and ASEAN in 1990s.

This cooperation involves areas of mutual gain for both sides which provides the impetus for the two (i.e. India and ASEAN) to form some kind of linkage even if it is modest at this point.

The idea of an AFTA-India dialogue is already under way and both are formulating modality to ensure higher trade by safeguarding mutual interests. Both have understood that it is in each other's interest to pursue a AFTA-India linkages.[22] India has been a dialogue partner of ASEAN since 1995 and during their annual meetings issues such as regional security, trade, aid, investment and others have been on the agenda. The AFTA-India dialogue will move beyond the original dialogue process on economic issues, although it will not replace it. Such a dialogue would, it is expected, produce greater results for free trade between both the partners as they will be able to make more comprehensive arrangements (or greater "synergy" as it is often referred to).

ASEAN is interested in the experience of the other regional organizations that are more advanced, notably the EU and NAFTA, but it is often noted by the ASEAN members that the advantage of India is that it is a complementary, as opposed to a competing, partner and that it has a large body of technical knowledge in the creation of free trade. Dialogue with the EU and NAFTA does not currently appear to have the potential to move forward. The EU dialogue tends to revolve around political issues and wider human rights issues in Southeast Asia. The dialogue with NAFTA is hampered by perceived domestic restraints on American officials. The idea of on AFTA-NAFTA linkage failed to go further than a series of roundtable discussions and shows no sign of going further at this point - although the existence of the dialogue, as with the dialogue with the EU, makes greater harmonization of trading regimes possible in the future. The AFTA-India dialogue, therefore, remains a more promising linkage than ASEAN's relations with larger economic blocs.

(viii) Could India Gain from AFTA?

It has often been stated that the AFTA-India dialogue is being created for the mutual benefit of both sides: in fact without this incentive there would be no impetus to the negotiation. The advantages for India are perhaps straightforward, namely increased trade access. With a growing interest in trade with Asia and an ideological predisposition to trade liberalization, India will attempt to persuade ASEAN nations to lower barriers to trade at any reasonable opportunity.

For India there are a number of tangible benefit to a linkage with AFTA, and in 1999 two-way trade between ASEAN-5 and India approached US $ 8.3 billion which was US $2.2 billion in 1990. With GDP growth for most ASEAN countries is again picking up in the aftermath of financial crisis, there is enormous potential for Indian traders to enhance their export to the region. It is, however, the area of two-way investment that both sides feel can be improved. Improving investment would be further assisted by many of the contacts made at the business level and exchange of information about customs, product standards, human resources, competition policy and business and industrial law.

The proposed AFTA-India consultations may provide a function far greater than the aspects of trade and investment. The dialogue is another diplomatic channel with ASEAN in India's close relationship with ASEAN as a whole. In regional security, the ASEAN Regional Forum (ARF) has become the premier vehicle for the discussions of Asia-Pacific Security issues, and demonstrates the role that ASEAN has had, and will continue to have, in the overall security of this region.[23] It is important for India to secure close relations with the ASEAN nations, and the AFTA-India dialogue forges an important commercial dimension. Ultimately though, because of geography, ASEAN and India are bound together and it makes perfect sense that the two should form intimate political, security, trade and investment links.

Table 5.1
India's Export Growth Rate with ASEAN-5 Countries
1992 to 1999

(Percentage)

	1992	*1993*	*1994*	*1995*	*1996*	*1997*	*1998*	*1999*	*Average 1992-95*	*Average 1996-99*
India's overall export rate	3.5	9.5	19.4	26.2	5.9	2.9	10.5	6.4	14.65	6.4
India's export growth rate with ASEAN-5										
Indonesia	–1.4	40.0	27.0	98.0	13.6	4.8	–8.9	–2.8	41.0	1.7
Malaysia	9.4	4.5	7.8	42.0	28.7	15.5	–24.4	20.8	15.9	10.2
Philippines	20.3	–37.7	98.0	28.4	42.6	40.8	–47.3	–6.2	38.0	7.5
Singapore	33.4	41.2	1.5	9.5	16.9	–5.4	–38.0	21.52	21.4	–1.3
Thailand	21.6	31.4	17.6	23.3	–5.9	6.0	–21.1	5.5	23.5	–3.9

Source : IMF "Direction of Trade Statistics Yearbook" – relevant issues.

Table 5.2

Intra-ASEAN-5 Export Trade Matrix (annual average)

1992-95 and to 1996-99

(US $ million)

Import / Export	Indonesia		Malaysia		Philippines		Singapore		Thailand		Total ASEAN-5		World	
	1992-95	1996-99	1992-95	1996-99	1992-95	1996-99	1992-95	1996-99	1992-95	1996-99	1992-95	1996-99	1992-95	1996-99
Indonesia	—	—	712	1413	348	683	3642	5573	483	833	5185	8502	38944	53583
Malaysia	684	1171	—	—	555	1135	11687	14576	2068	2788	14994	19670	55077	78786
Philippines	72	147	206	980	—	—	583	1815	355	744	1216	3686	12976	27223
Singapore	N.A.	N.A.	15031	20028	1422	2635	—	—	5087	5532	21540	28195	88144	118763
Thailand	434	1042	1276	2130	248	734	5314	5656	—	—	7272	9562	43104	56686
Total ASEAN-5	1190	1360	17225	24551	2573	5187	21226	27620	7993	9897	50207	69615	238245	335041

Source: As per Table 5.1 here.

Note: (i) Philippines exports to Indonesia in 1996 and to Thailand in 1994 is not available.

(ii) Singapore's exports to Indonesia throughout the period is not available.

NOTES & REFERENCES

1. Ambatkar, Sanjay (2000), "The Quest For Looking East: Case Study of Indo-ASEAN Economic Linkages" in *Foreign Trade Review*, Vol. XXXV, Nos. 2 & 3.
2. Lloyd, P.J. (1994), "Intra-regional Trade in the Asian and Pacific region", in *Asian Development Review*, vol.12, no.2.
3. The Countries signing the AFTA agreement were Brunei, Indonesia, Malaysia, Philippines, Singapore and Thailand.
4. ESCAP (1997), 'Implementations of the APEC process for Intra-regional trade and investment Flows', United Nations, Geneva.
5. De Rosa, Dean A. (1995), *Regional Trading Arrangements among Developing Countries: The ASEAN Example,* International Food Product Research Institute, Washington, D.C., USA.
6. Bowles, Paul (1997), "ASEAN, AFTA and the New Regionalism," in *Pacific Affairs*, Vol. 70, No.2.
7. Malaysia in mid-1990s mooted a new plan of East Asian Economic Caucus (EAEC) to be formulated by some of the ASEAN and North East Asian Countries such as Japan and S. Korea for greater regional cooperation in the matter of foreign investment.
8. Viner, Jacob (1950), *The Customs Union Issue*, Aderson Kramer Associates, Washington, D.C., USA.
9. De Melo, Jaime, and A. Panagariya (1993), (ed.), *New Dimensions in Regional Integration*', Cambridge University Press, USA.
10. Krugman, Paul (1991), *Geography and Trade* Leuven University Press, Belgium and MIT Press, Cambridge, USA.
11. Bhagwati, Jagdish (1997), "Regionalism Versus Multilateralism" in V.N. Balsubramanyam (ed.), *Jagdish Bhagwati's Writings on International Economics,* Oxford University Press, New Delhi.
12. De Melo and A. Panagariya (ed.), *op. cit.*
13. Krueger, A.O. (1999), *Regionalism and Multilaterialism in International Trade*, NCAER, New Delhi.
14. De Rosa, Dean A. *op. cit.*
15. Ariff, Mohamed (1997), "Intra-regional Trade Liberalization in ASEAN: A La AFTA" in *ASEAN in the New Asia—Issues and Trends*, Chia Siow Yue & Marcellow Pacini, (eds.), Institute of Southeast Asian Studies, Singapore.
16. Lim, Hank (1998), "ASEAN's International Competitiveness" in *ASEAN Towards 2020: Strategic Goals and Future Directions*, Stephen Leong,(ed.), ASEAN Academic Press Ltd., London.

17. The similar views were forecasted by Gerald Tan in 1982 through an empirical study entitled 'Trade Liberalization in ASEAN' brought out by Institute of Southeast Asian Studies, Singapore in series under Research Notes and Discussions Paper No. 32.
18. Frankel, Jeffrey A. (1997), *Regional Trading Blocs in the World Economic System,* Institute for International Economics, USA.
19. Plummer, Michael G. (1997), "ASEAN and the Theory of Regional Economic Integration - a survey" in *ASEAN Economic Bulletin,* Vol. 14, No. 2.
20. Petri, Peter A. (1997), "AFTA and the Global Track" in *ASEAN Economic Bulletin,* Vol. 14, No.2.
21 Thang, Nguyen Xuan (1998), "AFTA and ASEAN FDI in Vietnam" in *ASEAN: Today and Tomorrow,* National Political Publishing House, Hanoi, Vietnam.
22. Severino, Rodolfo C. (2001), '*ASEAN and India: A Partnership For Our Time,* Lecture delivered on January 9, 2001, at New Delhi under the Series of Eminent Persons Lecture.
23. India is a member of ARF and participates in all official meetings of the ARF. The ARF is a regional forum which looks into security aspect of Asia-Pacific region.

6

Challenges, Emerging Trend and Prospects for Cooperation

The world has now entered into the 21st century with much expectations from the Asia region. Experts see that many of the developing Asian economies may become developed one by the turn of half way mark of this century. There are forecasts and estimates about the future of global economy. The common thread in such estimates is that developed economies, specifically Japanese and European Union, would continue to face recession for the next five to ten years. Despite deployment of massive programme of structural reforms in the economies of Japan and European Union (EU), no sustained recovery is yet in sight. Recovery in Japan would depend upon fiscal (stimulating) policies. Owing to widespread excess capacity and weak balance sheets in the private sector, Japanese government outlays do not generate strong secondary effects.

In the case of EU, its 11 member countries are facing internal challenges with the adoption of a single currency, the euro. The EU has projected the euro as a competitor to the dollar. Contrary to their expectations it has depreciated by over 10 per cent since its introduction in early 1999, giving a much needed boost to European competitiveness but raising doubts about its credibility.[1] Even in case of USA the growth is likely to be moderate in coming days because of internal problems of employment and sagging domestic private demand.

In Asia, the pace and sustainability of the current economic recovery against the shadow of the July 1997 Asian meltdown is uncertain. The speedy recovery would depend upon how the crisis stricken economies of ASEAN and East Asian adopt measures to accelerate their growth rates. There is possibility that in coming days China may face the problem of maintenance of the exchange rate. The Asian crisis has led to the slackening of China's exports and domestic private demand. India marginally picked up GDP growth rate to 6.5 per cent in 1999 and export growth rate 11 per cent, however this recovery is not adequate for rapid development.

Given the persistent recession in industrial economies and slow recovery in Asian economies, a question can be asked - what would be the future paradigm of economic development for global economy? The development policy would be defined and implemented by taking into consideration two main forces: globalization (the continuing integration of the countries of the world); and liberalization (reduction in the trade barriers of the countries for free flow of trade transactions). The world is no longer a collection of relatively autonomous neighbourhood that are only marginally connected (by trade, for instance) and are generally immune to event in other neighbourhood. Information and ideas can be accessed in all corners of the globe at the push of a button. The international economic order is evolving into a highly integrated and electronically networked systems. So closely interwoven are financial markets that exchange rates, interest rates, and stock prices are intimately linked, and the amount of private capital circulating in financial markets dwarfs the resources of many countries.[2]

Another force of development policy is liberalization of trade regime. Future trade policy of countries would require a forward-looking agenda for broader trade liberalization mainly because development would lie in opening markets. Foreign trade has grown more quickly than the world economy in recent years and this trend is likely to continue. For developing countries, trade is the primary vehicle for realizing the benefits of globalization. Imports bring additional competitions and variety of domestic markets, benefiting consumers, and exports enlarge foreign markets benefiting businesses.

If developed countries reduce trade barriers in agriculture and services it would help developing countries to enhance their trade immensely. Trade in agricultural products is one area that offers many developing economies real opportunities. Trade in services is another issue which is speedily marching ahead in world trade and developing countries can outsmart developed countries in services sector. Driven by advances in information and communications technology, trade in services is growing explosively and developing countries can readily supply many sought-after services. India and ASEAN on the basis of their achievement in information technology are well poised to enhance bilateral interaction in services sector.

Challenges before ASEAN and role India can play

India's economic partnership with ASEANs in coming years will depend upon two factors: first, how the ASEAN states will address various challenges which they are currently facing individually and collectively; and secondly, how much significance the region will impart to India in resolving these challenges.[3] The first and foremost challenge before ASEAN today is of restructuring and rebuilding their economies in the aftermath of financial crisis. Notwithstanding their initial achievement (in the post-crisis period) in regaining partial momentum in GDP growth rate, much remains to be achieved, particularly in accelerating export growth rate. For this purpose, rebuilding of various sectors such as manufacturing with updated technology and skilled human resources is quintessential. Along with this, other sectors such as banking and finance need massive revamping in order to restore confidence of foreign investors. Equally important is restructuring of basic institutions like judiciary, bureaucracy to ensure transparency in government functioning. On the side lines of this, reform in political system with provision for establishment of democratic pattern of government is need of the hour. Because free market economy must move with democracy.[4]

Secondly, ASEAN faces a problem of lack of corporate power in the international arena and this continues to be one of the major constraints in their pursuit of achieving collective and individual diplomatic goals. A very few regional corporate companies dominate the world economic scene and because of this ASEAN faces a challenge of technology upgradation and creating knowledge - based human resources. The ASEAN success is currently dependent on borrowed technology from the industrialised nations however, to sustain economic prosperity for longer period, the region would require to develop its own technological capabilities as competent which would be that of advanced countries.

Thirdly, ASEAN's rapid economic progress during 1980s through 1990s was mainly owing to being ahead in the world in pushing for free market economic policies and trying to get foreign investment. But today, virtually every country has opened up and the world has become much more competitive. In such world ASEAN would find it difficult to maintain the same attractiveness of their economies. In its neighbourhood, China has already become the "favourite host" to large foreign investment and in a way has become "arch competitor" to the ASEAN.

Fourthly, the competitive industrial and trade structure between China and Southeast Asian economies like Indonesia, Vietnam, Thailand and to a lesser extent Malaysia, as well as the strategy of Japan, in integrating southeast Asia into its regional industrial division of labour, in order to sustain its global competitiveness despite the high yen, could lead to intensifying Japan-China rivalry playing out in Southeast. Japan's capital surplus status, strong industrial and technological base as well as its dependence on energy and raw materials make it very complementary with the ASEAN economies. While Japan's interest would be in maintaining its position as the head goose in the harmonious flying-geese pattern, with Southeast Asian nations like Thailand, Vietnam, Indonesia, and Malaysia subsumed under an informal regional trade and investment grouping, China is bound to context this pyramidal industrial structure and possibly use the powerful and pervasive overseas Chinese business groups in these countries to integrate Southeast Asian economies to the expanding China market to moderate the Japanese influence and prevent Japan from "Japanisation" of the ASEAN economies. The active cultivation of the Malaysian and Thai political and business group in recent period by China could be an indication of this emerging trend.[5]

Fifthly, the end of cold war era has posed a geopolitical challenge to the region. During cold war era, there were two fixed poles (i.e. US and USSR) in the world and ASEAN manouvered itself well within these two fixed poles. Today although US is seen as a unilateral pole but other nations such as China is trying to emerge as new power, if not in world, then in Asia. This has triggered many trecherous cross currents in present day world and this situation may create difficulties for ASEAN to manouvere smoothly.[6] Despite repeated assurances by China to its Asian neighbours regarding its belief in multipolar world and practising of the principle of non-zero-sum game, until lately the country is hardly successful in eliminating fears of "China threat" to ASEAN countries mainly because the country is engaged in stock-piling to huge nuclear (military) capability. Moreover, in recent past it has displayed inimical gestures towards Taiwan and has not washed its hands of an "expansionist" agenda.[7]

ASEAN's position in the Asia-Pacific region will mostly depend upon how ASEAN diplomatically handles China in engaging it in constructive partnership. Because it is estimated that by the year 2020 China will have most of the attributes of a regional hegemony and may attempts to become "middle Kingdom" in the region. China's assuming military power may sow the seeds of uncertainty in Asia and the prospects for ASEAN's transformation into a truly peaceful regional community may not be promising.[8] China's acquiring of military strength coupled with ascendancy of Chinese nationalism in recent period creates suspicion about the country's design towards ASEAN.

The presence of these challenges have turned the region a lot more complex. The recent financial crisis and the expansion of ASEAN forum itself are partly considered as responsible for this complexity. In addition ASEAN faces challenges from the changing nature of international finance, different practices of international relations since the end of the cold war, and the growth of civil society in member countries. Of course, ASEAN is addressing the issues, but it needs to do more to sustain in the mainstream of the world affairs.[9] To overcome these challenges ASEAN is applying regional and cooperative solutions as these problems are more and more regional and common in scope. For instance, ASEAN has responded to the financial crisis with greater solidarity. There could be two ways to address these problems: first by displaying stronger commitment to economic openness in the backdrop of financial crisis; and secondly by moving towards faster and closer economic integration within the region.[10] To address the security challenges the ASEAN needs to adopt the strategy of "cooperative security", meaning engagement of super powers in constructive economic partnership. It would be the arduous task of region's leadership to urge upon super powers to maintain indivisibility of peace and security in the region because peace is a necessary condition for development. Obviously it would be a "balancing act" on the part of region's leadership as each of these super powers have different motives and approaches towards the region.[11]

Given these wide-ranging challenges, India needs to sort out comprehensive strategy by giving equal significance to issues concerning economic, geopolitics, and security. ASEAN's economic partnerships with India goes beyond region's economic interests as it finds in India a mature Asian neighbour with immense potential to emerge as a major power on Asia map in coming years. It necessarily implies that ASEANs do not look at India as a "balancing power" to counter other powers in the region. But it also underscores the fact that ASEANs understand the significance of India being their partner in more than one way and expect that India must remain "engaged" in the region. The widespread appreciation of India's "look-east" policy by the entire region can be seen as a pointer in this direction and hence it all depends upon India how it consolidates its position in the region.[12]

Emerging Trend in Cooperation : India and ASEAN

Trade issues

The trade deficit of India with ASEAN-5 countries may be of concern to Indian government but this deficit has reduced in 1992-98 over the earlier period of 1985-91. Moreover out of five ASEAN countries India enjoys trade surplus with Indonesia, Philippines, and Thailand and accrues trade deficit with Malaysia and Singapore. Thus even in trade deficit there is silver lining and what is greater important is market access than trade imbalance. Initially, with the increase in exports, the imports would also increase and if country's foreign exchange reserves are in good position, the economy need not worry of rising imports. Currently India's overall forex reserves are adequate to meet the challenges of trade deficit and proportion of current account deficit (on balance of payments account) to GDP is within manageable limit.

The commodity structure of India-ASEAN-5 trade has undergone marked changes, specifically, India's switch from exporting mainly primary commodities to manufactured products. As the pace of rapid development of manufacturing sectors would continue in next several years, more efforts on the part of India to expand distant and relatively less penetrated ASEAN markets (so far) could be made. Other important thing to be noted is that demand for Indian information technology (IT) products in ASEAN markets is growing and the country is well poised to enhance exports of these products.

The access to ASEAN markets and more specifically to ASEAN-5 markets, may become even more significant to India as these countries are essentially "export oriented" and manufactured exports (of India) may be crucial to their growth strategies. It seems that in its trade relations with various ASEAN countries between 1985 and 1998 India could rapidly diversify the markets for its exports. Likewise, it had also diversified its sources of imports, thereby benefiting the ASEAN-5 countries. Of course, over the period India exported much less to ASEAN-5 than might be expected from India. Also India could have imported much more from ASEAN-5. Given relatively very low level of trade between India and ASEAN-5 compared to India's trade with third countries like USA and Japan; indeed the scope for further expansion of India-ASEAN-5 trade is considerable.

To enhance two-way trade of India-ASEAN there is need to look into tariff structure between two. India is still considered highly protected market and tariff rates are higher than international tariff standard. Since 1995 persistent efforts are on to bring down these rates and the tariffs are lowered down to great extent, however still there is room to reduce them further. With ASEAN, through mutual agreement, India can initiate process of lowering tariffs. In his recent visit to India between January 18 and 23, 2000, the Singaporean prime minister expressed that efforts should be made to create an 'Asian Free Trade Area', and India should take lead role in such attempts.[13] The implicit meaning of this appeal is that the ASEAN countries find India a highly protected regime and for enhancing interaction steps should be taken to unshackle trade regime. The onus of increasing trade lies with India and once the trade regime widely opens up, the economy may receive higher doses of FDI from ASEAN-5. Likewise, ASEAN-5 should reciprocate cooperatively in terms of their protective structures against Indian exports.

Such trade liberalization measures would have beneficiary welfare effect in India as imported goods would be cheaper thereby benefiting consumers, reducing inflation and stimulating domestic structural changes. Should employment in certain sectors in Indian economy be reduced with trade liberalization, it should also be remembered that ASEAN continues to offer a very substantial and rapidly growing market for Indian exports of both consumer and capital goods. Eventually, the gains from trade creation can stimulate the development of new and more productive industries in India capable of generating much greater employment opportunities.

Investment Issues

Both India and ASEAN (barring Singapore) are well-endowed with natural resources. Such industries which require tropical raw materials and other natural resources, as can be obtained in the ASEAN countries, offer certain "location specific advantages" which may be very attractive to Indian firms. Additional "locational advantages" for Indian firms and multinationals seeking sources, low labour cost can also be found in the labour- abundant countries like Philippines, Vietnam, Laos and Cambodia. Besides, very favourable fiscal and other incentives devised by government policies of ASEAN countries are offered to investors as these host countries compete with one another for foreign investments in consonance with their development priorities.[14] Moreover the outputs from the operations of Indian firms within ASEAN are advantageously located to serve the populous and increasingly affluent markets of ASEAN as well as the large markets of the Asia-Pacific Region.

India too offers various opportunities to ASEAN investors. The country is not only rich in natural resources but possesses a large pool of skilled and scientific human resources in various field. India's leap forward in engineering, medical, bio-technology, space-science, is well recognized as large no. of trained Indian personnel are working in different corners of the world including ASEAN region. Recently some ASEAN countries have entered into collaboration with India to take advantage of Indian expertise in knowledge-based industries. To cite few examples of India-ASEAN collaboration we can mention that in March 1999, eight ASEAN scientists underwent a one month attachment training in Hyderabad, Andhra Pradesh as part of the collaboration with their Indian counterparts in two advanced materials projects. Besides, in 1999 India conducted a programme to train ASEAN computer experts in advanced information technology. The National Institute of Information Technology (NIIT) of India conducted the training for about 100 trainees from ASEAN and for next few years this programme will continue. This was the first operational step towards establishment of the proposed ASEAN-India Information Training Centre in ASEAN.[15]

Future Prospects

The importance, present or prospective, of ASEAN to India and vice-versa, need not be further reiterated. The sentiments of ASEAN about India can be found in the appeal of the Singaporean Prime Minister urging India to reinforce and firm-up "look-east policy" and expand economic linkages with ASEAN.[16] India must see this appeal in right earnestness, especially in the backdrop of the Asian crisis and utilize every forum to enhance diplomatic and economic relationship.

What could be the modalities for increasing their proximity? The first and foremost is the trade and enlarged trade between them. On India's part, exports of value-added agricultural products (along with manufactured goods) could be one of the instruments to penetrate deeply ASEAN market. India's prospects in increasing exports of agricultural products to ASEAN is based on four factors: changes in ASEAN consumer habits, reductions in air transportation costs with the operation of private air liners, advances in the research field of India's biotechnology, and the liberalization of global trade rules.[17]

Besides, India can boost up trade in services with ASEAN. With the advent of electronic commerce trade in services world over would overtake trade in goods. In case of some of the ASEAN countries such as Singapore, Thailand, Malaysia services sector is prominent and these countries are known for exporting quality services. The ASEAN countries always demand further opening up of India's services and India must pay attention to ASEAN demand considering long term benefits. Thus trade emerges as the engine of enhancing interaction between India and ASEAN, and larger trade would lead to larger investment to follow. This prescription may sound contrary to popular perception that trade follows investment but in case of relations between India and ASEAN trade will pave way for ASEAN investment in India.

Opening the trade sector is crucial to attract higher doses of FDI from ASEAN. The reason is that foreign owned companies aiming for global competitiveness and international markets mostly go for larger investment outside local boundaries. FDI is now increasingly more connected with trading opportunities than local market exploitation. For instance, the huge increase in FDI in Mexico after the NAFTA came into force is evidence that the country is seen as a desirable base for supplying the US market. Of course, the presence of advanced infrastructure is equally important to attract sizeable amount of FDI. India needs to expedite the process of improving overall status of infrastructure for gaining larger foreign investment.

To sum up the prospects of enhancing economic interaction between India and ASEAN lies in understanding significance of each other beyond their mutual economic interests. The "look-east policy" provided an opportunity to both to move closer in more than one way and in a way created foundation for stronger ties in coming future. India's recent initiative in November 2000 in creating "Ganga-Mekong Suvarnabhumi Project" involving five ASEAN countries namely, Mynamar, Laos, Cambodia, Vietnam, and Thailand, lying on the banks of Indian river-Ganga and Southeast Asian river Mekong, may help in boosting economic interaction with these countries. Especially, it would help to provide impetus to reach out those countries which are so far relatively less represented in India's trade and investment transactions. Further, on February 13, 2001 India inaugurated 160-km long Tamu-Kalemyo road, linking India and Myanmar. This road may prove a key cross-border link to Myanmar as a part of India's policy to draw physical linkages with Southeast Asia. These efforts demonstrate India's commitment to "look-east policy" and earnestness to make it successful. Her attempts may get momentum provided the entire Southeast Asia reciprocates in similar way. Perhaps the world would be different in the 21st century if India and ASEAN could succeed in converging their respective "Vision 2020" and march together beyond the year 2020 by drafting "Shared Asian Vision".

NOTES & REFERENCES

1. UNCTAD, (1999), *Trade and Development Reports, 1999*, by UN, Geneva.

2 World Bank (1999), *World Development Report*, Washington DC, USA.

3. Ambatkar, Sanjay (2001) "India-ASEAN: Emerging Scenario in Economic Interaction" in *India Quarterly*, Vol. LVII, Nos. 1&2.

4. Kunio, Yoshihara (1999), *Building a Prosperous Southeast Asia: From Ersatz to Echt Capitalism*, Curzon Press, U.K.

5. Yam, Tan Kong (1997) "ASEAN in New Asia: Challenges and opportunities" in *ASEAN in the New Asia - issues and trends*, Chia Siows Yue and Marcellow Pacini (eds.), Institute of Southeast Asian Studies, Singapore.

6. Mahbubani, Kishore (1998), "ASEAN Towards 2020 : Strategic Goals and Critical Pathways" in *ASEAN Towards 2020: Strategic Goals and Future Direction*, Stephen Leong (eds.), ASEAN Academic Press Ltd., London.

7. Cheng, Joseph Y.S. (1999), "China's ASEAN Policy in the 1990s: Pushing for Regional Multipolarity" in *Contemporary Southeast Asia*, Vol. 21, No. 2.

8. Paribatra, Sukhumbhand (1998), "A Peaceful ASEAN Community: Milestone for the future" in *ASEAN Towards 2020: Strategic Goals and Future Directions* Stephen Leong (eds.), ASEAN Academic Press Ltd., London.

9. Funston, John (1999), "Challenges Facing ASEAN in a More Complex Age" in *Contemporary Southeast Asia*, Vol. 21, No. 2

10. Severino, Rodolfo (1998), "ASEAN at a Time of Change," ASEAN Secretariat, Jakarta, Indonesia.

11. Nathan, K.S. (1999) (ed.), *North America and the Asia-Pacific in the 21st Century: Challenges and Prospects for Cooperative Security and Prosperity*, ASEAN Academic Press Ltd., U.K.

12. Severino, Rofolfo, C. (2001) (Secretary-General, ASEAN), "ASEAN and India: A Partnership For Our Time" Lecture delivered on January 9, 2001 at New Delhi under the series of Eminent Persons Lecture.

13. *The Hindu* (newspaper), 'An interview of Mr. Goh Chok Tok, the Singapore Prime Minister, on his visit to India, New Delhi, January 22, 2000.

14. Recently the ASEAN countries announced programme of Investment Bold Measures, which is open to all investors, ASEAN and non-ASEAN. The programme includes a minimum 3 years corporate income-tax exemption or a minimum 30 per cent corporate investment tax allowance; 100 per cent foreign equity ownership; duty-free imports of capital goods; domestic market access; minimum industrial land lease-hold period of 30 years; employment of foreign personnel, and speedy custom clearance.
15. ASEAN Secretariat (1999), *ASEAN Annual Report, 1998-99* Jakarta, Indonesia.
16. *Ibid.*, 3.
17. Ambatkar, Sanjay (2000), "Modalities For Convergence of Economic Interests between India and ASEAN" in *Indian Ocean Digest*, Vol. 15, No. 1.

References

Ambatkar, Sanjay (1996) "Introduction" in *India and ASEAN: Economic Partnership in the 1990s and Future Prospects,* Ambatkar, et al. (edt.) Gyan Publishing House, New Delhi, pp.13-18.

Ambatkar, Sanjay (2002), "Trade-led strategy of India in ASEAN" in *Margin,* issue of January to March.

Ambatkar, Sanjay (2001), "Trends in Foreign Investment Interaction between India and ASEAN in 1990s" in *Paradigm,* Vol. 5, No. 1.

Ambatkar, Sanjay (2000), "The Quest for Looking East: Case Study of Indo-ASEAN Economic Linkages" in *Foreign Trade Review,* Vol. XXXV, Nos. 2 & 3.

Ambatkar, Sanjay (2001), "India-ASEAN: Emerging Scenario in Economic Interaction" in *India Quarterly,* Vol. LVII, Nos. 1 & 2.

Ambatkar, Sanjay (2000), "Modalities for Convergence of Economic Interests between India and ASEAN" in *Indian Ocean Digest,* Vol. 15, No. 1.

Ariff, Mohamed (1997), "Intra-regional Trade Liberalization in ASEAN: A La AFTA" in *ASEAN in the New Asia—issues and trends,* Chia Siow Yue & Marcellow Pacini, (eds.), Institute of Southeast Asian Studies, Singapore.

ASEAN Secretariat World Wide Website<http://www asean

ASEAN Secretariat, *ASEAN Annual Report,* Jakarta, Indonesia, various issues of relevant years.

Bhagwati, Jagdish (1997), "Regionalism Versus Multilateralism" in V.N. Balsubramanyam (ed.)- *Jagdish Bhagwati's Writings on International Economics,* Oxford University Press, New Delhi.

Bowles, Paul (1997), "ASEAN, AFTA and the New Regionalism" in *Pacific Affairs,* Vol. 70, No.2.

Cheng, Joseph Y.S. (1999), "China's ASEAN Policy in the 1990s:

Pushing for Regional Multipolarity" in *Contemporary Southeast Asia*, Vol. 21, No. 2.

De Melo, Jaime, and A. Panagariya (1993), (ed.), *New Dimensions in Regional Integration*, Cambridge University Press, USA.

De Rosa, Dean A. (1995), *Regional Trading Arrangements among Developing Countries: The ASEAN Example*, International Food Product Research Institute, Washington, D.C., USA.

DGCI & S, *Foreign Trade Statistics of India - Principal Commodities* and Countries', Calcutta, India, various issues of relevant years.

Ding Lu and Zhu Gangti (1995), "Singapore FDI in China-Features and Implications" in *ASEAN Economic Bulletin*, Singapore, Vol. 12, No. 1, pp. 53-63.

ESCAP (1997), *Implementations of the APEC process for Intra-regional trade and investment Flows*, United Nations, Geneva.

Frankel, Jeffrey A. (1997), *Regional Trading Blocs in the World Economic System*, Institute for International Economics, USA.

Funston, John (1999), "Challenges Facing ASEAN in a More Complex Age" in *Contemporary Southeast Asia*, Vol. 21, No. 2.

Gough, Leo (1998), *Asia Meltdown: The end of the Miracle?* - Capstone Publishing Limited, U.K.

IMF, *Direction of Trade Statistics Yearbook* - various issues of relevant years.

Indian Investment Centre, *Indian Joint Ventures and Wholly Owned Subsidiaries Abroad*, New Delhi, various issues of relevant years.

Jalan, Bimal (1997), *India's Economic Policy-Preparing for 21st Century*, Penguin Books, New Delhi, p.p. 91-106.

Jomo, K.S. (1998), "Malaysia: From Miracle to Debacle" in *Tigers in Trouble - Financial Governance, Liberalization and Crisis in East Asia*, Jomo, K.S. (ed.), Zed Books Ltd., UK.

Jomo, K.S. et al (1997), *Southeast Asia's Misunderstood Miracle: Industrial Policy and Economic Development in Thailand, Malaysia and Indonesia*, Westview Press, USA.

Keenan, Faith (1998), (ed.), *The Aftershock-How an Economic Earth-Quake is Rattling Southeast Asian Politics*, Review Publishing Company Ltd., Hong Kong.

Krueger, A.O. (1999), *Regionalism and Multilaterialism in International Trade*, NCAER, New Delhi.

Krugman, Paul (1991), *Geography and Trade*, Leuven University Press, Belgium and MIT Press, Cambridge, USA.

Krugman, Paul (1995), "The Myth of Asia's Miracle" in *Foreign Affairs*, 6(73), pp. 62-78.

Kunio, Yoshihara (1999), *Building a Prosperous Southeast Asia: From Ersatz to Echt Capitalism*, Curzon Press, U.K.

Lauridsen, Laurids S. (1998), "Thailand: Causes, Conduct, Consequences" in *Tigers in Trouble - Financial Governance, Liberalization and Crises in East Asia*, Jomo, K.S. (ed.), Zed Books, Ltd., U.K.

Lim, Hank (1998), "ASEAN's International Competitiveness" in *ASEAN Towards 2020: Strategic Goals and Future Directions*, Stephen Leong,(ed.), ASEAN Academic Press Ltd., London.

Lim, Joseph Y. (1998), "The Philippines and the East Asian Economic Turmoil" in '*Tigers in Trouble - Financial Governance, Liberalization and Crisis in East Asia*" Jomo, K.S. (ed.), Zed Book, Ltd., U.K.

Lloyd, P.J. (1994), "Intra-regional Trade in the Asian and Pacific region", in *Asian Development Review*, vol.12, no.2.

Mahbubani, Kishore (1998), "ASEAN Towards 2020: Strategic Goals and Critical Pathways" in *ASEAN Towards 2020: Strategic Goals and Future Direction*, Stephen Leong (eds.), ASEAN Academic Press Ltd., London.

Montes, Manuel (1998), *The Currency Crisis in Southeast Asia*'-Institute of Southeast Asian Studies, Singapore.

Montes, Manuel and M.A. Abdusalamov (1998), "Financial Crisis in Indonesia" in *Tigers in Trouble - Financial Governance, Liberalization and Crisis in East Asia*, Jomo, K.S. (ed.), Zed Books Ltd., U.K.

Nathan, K.S. (1999), (ed.), *North America and the Asia-Pacific in the 21st Century: Challenges and Prospects for Cooperative Security and Prosperity*, ASEAN Academic Press Ltd., U.K.

Paribatra, Sukhumbhand (1998), 'A Peaceful ASEAN Community: Milestone for the future" in *ASEAN Towards 2020: Strategic Goals and Future Directions*, Stephen Leong (eds.), ASEAN Academic Press Ltd., London.

Petri, Peter A. (1997) "Measuring and Comparing Progress in Apec" in *ASEAN Economic Bulletin*, Singapore, vol. 14, No. 1, pp. 1-13.

Petri, Peter A. (1997), "AFTA and the Global Track" in *ASEAN Economic Bulletin*, Vol. 14, No.2.

Plummer, Michael G. (1997), "ASEAN and the Theory of Regional

Economic Integration - a survey" in *ASEAN Economic Bulletin*, Vol.14, No.2.

Rachain Chintayarangson, et al. (1992), "ASEAN Economies, Macro-Economic Perspective" in *ASEAN Economic Bulletin* Singapore, Vol. 8, No. 3, pp. 353-375.

Rakshit, Mihir (1997), "Crisis, contagion and Crash: Asian Currency Turmoil" in *ICRA Bulletin: Money & Finance*, New Delhi, No.4, p.p. 8-45.

Rakshit, Mihir (1998), "Retracing the Roots of Asian Troubles 1996-97, Some analytical issues and empirical evidence" in *ICRA Bulletin: Money and Finance*, New Delhi, No.5, p. p. 7-41.

Rao, Bhanoji, V.V. (1996), "APEC and India: Emerging Linkages" in Ambatkar, et al (edt.) op. cit., p.p. 219-245.

Rasiah, Rajah (2000), "The Asian Financial Crisis and Recovery Plans" in *Southeast Asia Into the 21st Century: Crisis and Beyond* - A.R. Embong and J. Rudolph (ed.) - Penerbit University Kabangsaan Malaysia, Bangi, Malaysia.

Reddy, Y.V. (1998), *Asian Crisis : Asking the Right Questions, Lecture* delivered at India International Centre, New Delhi on May 1, 1998.

Reserve Bank of India (RBI), *Annual Reports*, Mumbai, India, various issues of relevant years.

Secretariat For Industrial Assistance, Govt. of India, *SIA Newsletter*, New Delhi, various relevant issues.

Severino, Rodolfo (1998), *ASEAN at a Time of Change* ASEAN Secretariat, Jakarta, Indonesia.

Severino, Rodolfo C. (2001) Secretary General, ASEAN, 'ASEAN and India- A Partnership For Our Time' Lecture delivered on January 9, 2001, at New Delhi under the Series of Eminent Persons Lecture.

Stiglitz, Joseph (1998), 'The East Asian Crisis and its Implications For India' Lecture delivered at Industrial Finance Corporation of India (IFCI), New Delhi on May 19, 1998.

Stiglitz, Joseph (1999), "Full Recovery Ahead" an interview in *Far Eastern Economic Review*, November 4, 1999.

Thang, Nguyen Xuan (1998), "AFTA and ASEAN FDI in Vietnam" in *ASEAN: Today and Tomorrow*, National Political Publishing House, Hanoi, Vietnam.

The Hindu (newspaper), An interview of Mr. Goh Chok Tong, the Singapore Prime Minister on his visit to India, New Delhi, January 22, 2000.

UNCTAD, *World Investment Report*, UN, Geneva, various issues of relevant years.

UNCTAD, *Trade and Development Report* UN, Geneva, - various issues of relevant years.

Viner, Jacob (1950), *The Customs Union Issue*, Aderson Kramer Associates, Washington, D.C., USA.

World Bank (1993), *The East Asian Miracle: Economic Growth and Public Policy*, Oxford University Press, New York, USA.

World Bank, *World Development Report*, Washington DC, USA, various issues of relevant years.

Yam, Tan Kong (1997) "ASEAN in New Asia: Challenges and opportunities" in *ASEAN in the New Asia - issues and trends* Chia Siows Yue and Marcellow Pacini (eds.), Institute of Southeast Asian Studies, Singapore.

Yamashita, Shochi (1998), "ASEAN Thirty Years on: Challenges and Problems to be solved" in *ASEAN: Today and Tomorrow*, National Political Publishing House, Hanoi, Vietnam.

Index

❑❑❑